HOOKED FOR LIFE

HOOKED FOR LIFE
BY JOE ULVELING

Hooked For Life

Copyright © 2011 by Joe Ulveling

ISBN: 978-0-9833181-0-1

Cover design by Jim Thorne & Steve Davenport

This book is lovingly dedicated
to my lifetime date and my wife...Debbie.

Thank you for helping me be the best
I can be for God and for our family.

Contents

Acknowledgements

I am very grateful for the many people who have encouraged me in various ways for this project. I'd like to thank my parents, Dr. & Mrs. Charles Ulveling, along with our ministry board members, Jim & Kathy Law and Steve & Lori Cannon.

I'd also like to express my appreciation to my mother-in-law, Mrs. Sherry Grinstead, Todd & Angela Ellett, and Angela Witcher for their input, time and editing assistance to make this book the best it can be. Ya'll helped me a ton!

I'm also deeply grateful to my wife, Debbie, for her many hours of editing, bouncing ideas back and forth, and listening to me run MANY ideas past her. Thank you!

Introduction

I'm just an average Joe. I was in the corporate world for several years before the Lord called me into family ministry, so I know what the "real" world is like. Many pressures can pull on us from the outside such as work, kid's ball games, church activities and many other things. A husband and wife can go through the motions for years and slowly drift apart. My heart is to help you with "average Joe" principles that you can apply and that can actually work in your marriage. Speaking of sharing our lives, I've been thinking about how we spend our time together, so check this out. What a wonderful milestone it is for a couple being married 50 years or more. Let's take a minute and dissect their time spent together: They will sleep together approximately 18,000 nights, eat about 36,000 meals together, and spend hundreds of holidays together and with family. (Now, I know what you ladies are thinking...you're thinking, "Man, Joe, that's a ton of dirty dishes for 36,000 meals!") The bottom line is this...if you're going to commit your life to your spouse and you're going to spend fifty years with them, then why not make it the absolute best that it can be? Why make it just an "existing together" relationship? If you're going to sleep together 18,000 nights, eat 36,000 meals together and spend hundreds of holidays together, why make it drudgery and just get by when it can be great? If you're committing your life to someone and then you just "exist", you are, in essence, wasting your life away. Marriage can be awesome with your best friend...your spouse!

PART ONE

WHAT IT TAKES
TO CATCH 'EM

IS WHAT IT TAKES
TO KEEP 'EM

Chapter 1

The Big Catch

I'd like to tell you a fishing story. It's a true fishing story, so don't laugh. My wife, Debbie, and I were out deep sea fishing with her sister and our brother-in-law off the coast of Pensacola, Florida. We were out about fifteen miles off the coast. We were out so far that you couldn't see land, and the boat was just rocking around...over and over and over. We were really feeling sick and green. Have you ever had that feeling before? It's awful! We were bottom fishing and catching a lot of fish. Scott got another fishing pole out, put a big bait fish on the end (bigger than most fish I had ever caught), threw it out as far as he could, locked it in and put the pole on top of the boat. I said Scott, "What are you doing?" He said, "I'm trying to catch a kingfish." After I heard the word "kingfish", I was hoping for the big one. We waited for a while and...zing...the line started being taken out. Isn't that such a sweet sound? He cranked on the line a couple of times and then handed the pole to me and said, "Here, Joe, you've never caught a kingfish before." I started cranking the reel as hard as I could. I decided that I was going to yank that fish inside the boat, right now! I wasn't sure what a kingfish was, but it sounded huge! I had determined in my mind that fish was not getting any line from me, and it's not taking any more drag or slack. I was going to bring that fish in on my terms.

It came in about half way and then it jumped out of the water; I didn't see it but Scott said, "It's a good sized one." WHOA! That just caused me to work all the harder at bringing it in. I was cranking away on that fishing reel as fast as I could. I was determined I was going to win this battle.

Now, have you ever seen the fishing shows where a guy has on a harness that's attached to the boat so the fish won't pull him in? I thought I was bringing in the "big one" and thought to myself, "Those guys are wimps". The fish started getting close to the boat and Scott got ready to help me bring it in. Suddenly, my line went slack, and the fish got away. That's when Scott said, "Joe, I forgot to tell you, the closer it gets, the more tender you have to be with it."

You know, in comparison, the closer our spouse gets the more tender we need to be with them. As we stand in our "boat of marriage," we tend to do what I did with that kingfish. We tend to think in terms of "it's my way, or the highway." We've got our spouses on the hook — we have our wedding rings on, but we try to yank them around in our "boat of marriage." If we try to yank them in, they're going to get away and get off of the hook. If we let them take all the line out where the line is slack, they're going to get off the hook that way too.

I can demonstrate this with a wet bar of soap. If I squeeze too tightly, it will slip right out of my hands. On the other hand, if I hold it too loosely, it will fall out of my hands. I have to have the right hold on that bar of soap to keep it in my hands.

So, what should I do everyday in my "boat of marriage"? Reel them in tenderly. Not too hard...and not too soft. It's not always those big things that you do, but the small thoughtful gestures you do for your spouse to keep them on the hook. It's the little things you do to show your spouse they are valuable to you. Its things like writing a note and putting it in their car to say you love them.

I saw a commercial on TV where a couple is standing in a courtyard in London. There are all kinds of birds, but mostly pigeons surrounding them. This man looks around and then yells for all to hear, "I love this woman!" He's hollering and she's kind of embarrassed and sheepishly looking around. Then he pulls out this big diamond ring and she hugs him and says "I love this man." It's not those big things, like the diamond ring, it's the little things we do everyday to keep our spouse hooked on us. What it takes to catch them is what it takes to keep them.

"...If you would treat your spouse like you were still on your honeymoon, regardless of how long you've been married, and do the things you did to win them over; you will have a thriving marriage!"

What did you do before marriage, while you were dating, to win them over? Those are the same things you need to do to keep them won over! **The bottom line is this...if you would treat your spouse like you were**

still on your honeymoon, regardless of how long you've been married, and do the things you did to win them over; you will have a thriving marriage!

As you read this book, you will make a decision to do one of two things: 1) Stay where you're at in your marriage, or 2) Make some changes. If you decide to stay where you are in your marriage, let me share with you where you may fall in some of these categories or statistics.

Studies show that almost half of all divorces take place within two to three years of the wedding day. Can you believe that? If you're a newlywed or engaged, this will really get your attention. So why does this happen? There's such a pressure cooker of adjustments and changes right at the beginning of a marriage. Real important things...like who's going to get what closet space, where are we going to go for the holidays, whose family are we going to spend the most time with, where are we going to eat dinner, and which way does the toilet paper hang on the roll...over or under? All of these small insignificant issues build and build and build until the kettle blows! So this is why building your marriage upon a strong foundation is essential! My goal is for you to not become a statistic in your marriage.

The statistics for divorce rates have varied depending on the data, but the bottom line is marriages are crumbling at an epidemic rate in our society. I'm thankful to be able to give you some hope at this point. Recent data shows that couples who are truly committed in their Christian walk attend church regularly, read their Bible faithfully, and pray together or individually have a reduced rate of divorce over someone who isn't faithful in these areas. An article by Glenn T. Stanton states, "Based on the best data available, the divorce rate among Christians is significantly lower than the general population." He further stated, "The divorce rates of Christian believers are not identical to the general population—not even close. Being a committed, faithful believer makes a measurable difference in marriage."[1] The point is this...our spiritual lives really do make a difference in our marriages and families.

If you were to take a bowl and drop it on your kitchen floor, it would shatter into thousands of pieces. It's virtually impossible to put that bowl back together. What a lot of people do is wait too long to get help. They wait until the problem is at its height and then they bring all of the pieces to a counselor or pastor and say, "Will you help us put the pieces back together?" When the bowl is shattered, a lot of times it's too late to get it back in shape. When the bowl has a crack in it, that's a good time to get help and fix it. At this point it's a lot easier to glue it back together, to repair it, to put it back in good order and make it strong like it needs to be. I believe that pride is what holds a lot of people back from getting help. They're afraid of what others will think. It doesn't matter what others think, it only matters what your Heavenly Father thinks about you! What's more important; what others think about you, or your marriage? Well, when you put it like that, it is easy to see your marriage is the most important. If you keep your marriage a priority, you won't choose to live in mediocrity. You'll want to improve yourself and your marriage.

Studies show people who live together before marriage have an increased chance of divorce. That's a message our teens and singles need to hear loud and clear. God's plan is not a trial run. God's plan is one man, one woman, for life. That's His plan for marriage.

You may decide to stay where you are and fall into these statistics, or you can make the decision to implement change. I hope you choose to implement change. When you started reading this book, you probably expected me to talk about some specific things. The guys are probably expecting me to talk about communication and 'sharing' by opening up and listening. We'll be talking about some of those things in a way you can understand them better. The ladies are probably expecting me to talk about sex. Yeah, we'll be talking about that, but in a way you can better understand your husband. (I'm sure when I say, "We'll be talking about sex", the guys will keep reading.)

This will be a time to step back, out of your busy life's bubble, like an annual review is with your job. When you have an annual review, you take a breath, slow down and take a look back and say "...what are my strengths, what are my developmental needs, what are some areas in which I'm doing well and need to continue to do?" That's what this time is about with regards to your marriage. You need to step away from your marriage and ask yourself, "What are some things we're doing well, what are our developmental needs and what do we need to work on in order to strengthen our relationship?"

Is your marriage thriving or existing? According to studies, Dr. James Dobson has reported that two out of ten marriages have a truly satisfied and bonded relationship. Guess what's happening to the other eight, or 80% of the people who are married? They're just existing, just making it from day to day. They're roommates who happen to live in the same house. They're roommates who just happen to share the same bed. They're roommates who happen to share meals together, who share the same tube of toothpaste. They're roommates but they don't really have anything in common. They're roommates who have children together. They don't really know the other person they've been spending all their time with. Some are experiencing great difficulty, when God intended marriage to be,"a little bit of heaven on earth". Marriages don't have to just exist. Marriages are made in heaven, but they must receive maintenance on earth.

"Before marriage, opposites attract; after marriage, opposites attack". Sometimes the very thing that attracted you to your spouse can drive you absolutely nuts after you get married. For example, say that one of you is very quiet, timid and shy, while your date is very outgoing. One thing you admire is how they can walk into a room and not be embarrassed or afraid to walk up to anybody and talk to them. The outgoing individual gets along with everybody. The one who is quiet sees that quality in the other person and says to themselves, "I wish I could be more like that." After marriage, that same person is saying, "Are they ever going to be quiet? I can't get them to stop talking." You don't realize some of those things until you're married. It's funny how that works.

"It's my prayer that regardless of how different you and your spouse are, you'll learn to love them for who they are...not for what they could become if they lived up to your expectations."

It's OK that you and your spouse are different. In fact, it's a good thing because you help make each other stronger. You help balance each other out. It's my prayer that regardless of how different you and your spouse are, you'll learn to love them for who they are...not for what they could become if they lived up to your expectations. Love them right now and see what a huge difference it makes. Turn your focus onto them and off yourself. Let's work on having strong marriages and do what it takes to keep from existing in our lives and relationships. Let's journey on together as we come to the application time and then onto specific ways to stay, "Hooked for Life". I know you can do it!

Notes

1. Glenn T. Stanton, "The Christian divorce rate myth (what you've heard is wrong)", in Baptist Press News (www.bpnews.net), February 15, 2011.

Application Time

An application time is included at the end of each chapter. This is the time for you, as a couple, to talk about some of the things that were just covered in each chapter and apply them to your life. It is a very important time for you if you are trying to accomplish the goals necessary to improve your marriage. Keep in mind this exercise is not intended to cure everything in a marriage relationship. This exercise is meant to give you a "jump-start" with your spouse.

Have you ever had a dead battery in your car? I'm sure many of you have. What do you have to do to the car to get it going? First, you have to jump it with jumper cables. Once it's started, you let it run so it can charge itself up. Since the topic is marriage, "buying a new battery" is not an option. Once the battery has been jumped off, it has to charge up to get to full power. I am trying to provide marriage "jumper cables", and I am trying to give each of you a "charge or jump start." Once I have done that, I can't do the recharging. That's up to you as a couple. For a car battery, a speed charge damages the battery over the long haul. A slow charge allows the recharging process to complete the full cycle and works better in the long haul, but it takes time. This application time is a nudge to help get you moving in the right direction in your relationship.

Another tool to help you is the 1–10 scale. One is the lowest score and ten is the highest. If a couple indicates to me that their level of communication is awful, I would ask that couple to rank their communication on a scale of 1–10. Say this couple ranks it at a 2. My question to them is not, "What will it take to get to a 10?" Rather, my question to them is, "What will it take to get to a 3?" You must take things one step at a time. If you try to tackle too much at a time, you'll get discouraged. Be thankful for and celebrate the small improvements! If that couple returns and admits their communication still needs work, but that it is now at a 3, my question to them would be, "What will it take to get to a 4?" That couple comes up with their own solution, unique to them. After this exercise you will not be at a 10. Remember the car and recharging the battery? It's not going to charge up to the fullest capacity right away. It takes time. If you try to do too much, you'll hurt yourselves and feel defeated. Take it one step at a time.

This is the most important thing you will see in this book. Having a daily quiet time and praying together is the glue which will hold your marriage and family together! Open your Bible each day and say, "Lord, teach me and show me today what you would have me learn. Speak to my heart through your Word today." Write down a verse or a promise on a piece of paper. Put it in your pocket, so you can meditate on His word throughout the day. Pray together each day as husband and wife, and not just praying before your meal. I'm talking about a deliberate time when you pray together as a team. You need to make it a priority to pray with and for your spouse and family on a regular basis.

This next suggestion is specifically for men. I want to remind you again about the importance of a daily quiet time and praying with your wife. For the average man, the very thought of praying with his spouse puts fear and trembling into his body.

Most men are intimidated by the idea of praying with their wives. I certainly was. I remember my pastor, who I really looked up to, transparently shared about his prayer time with his wife. He said that he was scared and nervous when he started praying with his wife. I thought to myself, "I thought I was the only one who was scared to start praying with my wife. If my pastor of this huge church felt the same way, then it must mean I'm normal and that I'm 'okay' to feel this way". His honesty normalized this area in my life and gave me the courage to start praying with my wife as well. That was a real "light bulb" moment for me!

Even if you're used to praying in church or other venues, there's something different about praying with someone who knows you better than anyone else in the entire world. Your wife desperately wants you to be the spiritual leader of your home. Starting to pray with her is a huge step to being the spiritual leader in your home. She will look at you in a whole different way, and you will automatically go to a different level of leadership in her eyes. In time, this wonderful opportunity will become normal for you and, eventually, you will pray automatically and with more ease. This is my challenge to you: Start praying with your spouse even if you're not sure what to say. If you're not sure what to pray about, I've included a prayer topic below that will help to get you started. Ask your wife to close her eyes as you read this prayer. This is a great place to start fulfilling this challenge.

I believe the men in our churches are our greatest untapped resource. If we, as men of God, would take the lead, take charge, stand up, and be real; our churches, our families, and our nation would be SO strong! Most men wimp out and let others take the lead; so men, I'm calling you to action...stand up to be a real man of God, and be a strong husband for your wife as you lead her in this area.

Application Time

Reminisce about your dating days and when you met. What attracted you to each other?

. . . .
. . . .
. . . .
. . . .

What made you fall in love with your spouse?

. . . .
. . . .
. . . .
. . . .

What changes do you need to make to keep your spouse hooked on you?

. . . .
. . . .
. . . .
. . . .

Prayer Topic

Lord, thank you for allowing me to catch my spouse. Help me to focus on meeting his/her needs. Help me to remember and have that zeal I once had for my spouse. Help me to start treating my spouse with the same respect I once gave.

Chapter 2

Lures

What happens often in marriage is that by accident or deliberately, we take away the lure, or the bait, we used to catch our spouse. Let's look at four lures that we used to catch our spouse. We're going to see what it took to catch 'em with this lure, and then we'll look at what it takes to keep em' on the hook with this lure as well.

Looks

The first lure we use to catch our spouse is...Looks. Here's what it took to "catch 'em":

When you were first trying to catch your spouse, you wanted to look good. Ladies, how long did it take you to get ready for your first dates? It probably took you quite a while. If your hair didn't look just right, what would you do? You would wash it again and redo it. You would borrow someone's clothes or buy some new clothes. You would do whatever it took to look your very best for your dates. Here's my point — You wanted to look good for your prospective spouse, and you spent some time to make sure everything was perfect. I'm not trying to be superficial, but physical appearance is one of those things that first attracted you to your spouse.

In college, when I first met my wife, Debbie, she got my attention. I was on my way to baseball practice, and she was jogging with her friend, Terri. I knew Terri since she played softball, but I had never met Debbie before and I was too shy at the time to make the first move anyway. They stopped right in front of my dorm. Terri introduced us, and we chatted for a few minutes, and then they jogged away. Now, my first reaction was not, "Who was that...she's ugly...I'd like to spend more time with her!" No, my reaction was, "WOW, is she ever beautiful...I'd like to get to know her better!" My point is this — looks is one of those things that does attract us to our potential mate.

Here's how to keep 'em when it comes to looks. How much effort do you put into it now? How long does it take you to get ready now? Are you using the same effort you once did to stay attractive to your spouse?

Men and women are really different. Do you know how a guy finds clean clothes? First he picks it up off of the floor, and then he smells it. If it smells clean, it must be clean, so it's okay to wear!

Women are a little more complex. Debbie will be getting ready to go somewhere or getting ready for church. She'll ask me to choose which dress to wear of the two she's holding up. If I pick the dress in her right hand, then she'll usually end up wearing the one in her left hand. Why is that ladies? The shoes come after the dress. Debbie will come to me with two different pairs of shoes on. She'll lift up one leg like a flamingo, so I can see the shoe all by itself with the outfit. She then proceeds to do the same thing with the other shoe. After that comes the earrings and so on. I believe you've got the picture by now.

Ladies, here's an important point for you to remember. Men are stimulated by sight. Men are visual creatures. If you want to get your husbands' engines cranking, put on something that looks good to him. He'll be ready to go.

Ladies, since men are visual creatures, how do you look when your husband gets ready to go to work in the morning? Picture this...you have your flannel nightgown on, your comfy slippers on (You know those big fuzzy ones that are SO comfortable, but are SO ugly and everyone hates?), bed head, and teeth that aren't brushed. OK...you say to your husband as he's walking out, "Have a good day at work". As your husband walks away looking over his shoulder he thinks, "Yeah, I sure am glad I'm going to work. I hope she looks better before I get home." When he comes home, the only thing different is that you brushed your teeth and maybe got dressed. You still have the bed head, no make-up and the slippers on.

Women are emotional creatures. What they think, and how they feel are what gets their engines cranking. Gentlemen, if you want to get your wives' engines cranking, then you need to treat her well. She needs to know, not just in words, but in actions, that you truly value and love her. It's the small things you do such as helping to clean up after dinner, vacuum the house, tell your wife she looks very pretty, and helping with the children that let her know she's valued. Guys, when you show your wife you value her, her engine will start up, then it will idle, and soon it will be blaring all over the house, "VROOOOOM"!

Emotional Attachment

The second lure we use to catch our spouse is…Emotional Attachment. Here's what it took to "catch 'em" on an emotional level:

When you were dating, your whole desire was to fulfill their every need. Your whole world revolved around them. You treated them with utmost respect. You valued your date, and everything they said was valued. You respected their dreams, their thoughts, and their beliefs. You couldn't get enough of them. You hung on their every word.

Here's the point when it comes to emotional attachment; You valued your date. When they talked, you listened because you valued what they had to say. By treating them this way, it builds up an emotional attachment, or bond, between you, and that attachment extends into your marriage as husband and wife. You met their every need, want and desire and were extremely happy to do so. This kind of emotional security breeds a sense of security and safety. It makes your relationship a "safe" place to address issues and share your life together.

Here's what it takes to keep 'em when it comes to emotional attachment. What are your actions saying now? Are you still treating your spouse in that same special way? Do you hang on their every word with respect? Do you value them like you once did to build an emotional attachment? After marriage, the tendency is to become focused on yourself instead of your spouse. Where is your focus?

Let me give you two examples I think will help you as we proceed with this. In the first example, reminisce back to your dating days. Ladies you're talking on the phone with your date. You say, "Boy, my car sure is dirty; it's filthy and needs to be washed." The guy's response is, "I can do that! I'll be over there, and I'll hand wash it, hand wax it, clean the inside, armor all the tires and I'll put air freshener on the inside. Just tell me what you want; cherry, piña colada, strawberry, or banana. I can be there in eight-to-nine minutes, to get your car and I'll clean it up for you." Who is this guy focused on—himself or his soon-to-be spouse? Yes, he is focused on her.

In the second example, this same couple has now been married for a few years. They're having the same conversation. The wife says, "My car sure is dirty; it's filthy and needs to be washed." The guy's response is a little different now; "Do it yourself, you've got two good arms, and two good legs. It'll be good exercise for you. Did you forget where the car wash is? Do you need some money?" Who is this guy focused on? He's focused on himself. It's a funny thing in marriage where we would once do anything for our spouse, and now our response is, "Do it yourself". This example plays out for both men and women, not just men. It becomes an area of selfishness. I think you could agree with me that a lot of times married couples change their focus from what they once would do for their spouse to "get them on the hook" to how they act now. We need to go back to the focus we once had to keep them on the hook when it comes to emotional attachment.

The best example I can give you comes out of the Bible in Ephesians 5. "Husbands, love your wives, just as Christ also loved the church and gave Himself up for her." Eph 5:25 (NASB)

This passage talks about how Jesus loved the church and gave Himself for her. There's no greater love than what Jesus Christ did by laying down His life for you and for me. When a man thinks about how Jesus loved the church and gave Himself for her, the first thing he says to himself is that he would put himself in harm's way to protect his spouse. When Jesus died on the cross, he willingly died for you, for me, and for the entire world. He died for everyone. Wow, that's a true demonstration of love! The most important decision anyone can make in their life is accepting Jesus into their heart and believe what Jesus Christ did on the cross and say, "Lord, I accept you into my heart and life to be my personal Lord and Savior." You need to know you've had a specific time in your

"Your marriage and your Christian walk shouldn't be about yourself, but about others."

life when you accepted Jesus Christ into your heart and gave Him your life. The point is this...when Jesus Christ died on the cross, whose needs did he put first? Ours or his? He put our needs first. So, when Jesus died on the cross, he willingly died for us. When he was here on earth serving, was he here for himself or for others? He was here for others. Our Christian life is not about ourselves, but it's about others. In our marriages, it's not about ourselves, but it's about others...our spouse. Do you see the analogy now and how these two are tied together? I hope this will help you as you think about this area in your marriage. Your marriage and your Christian walk shouldn't be about yourself, but about others. If you don't show your spouse you value them, chances are someone else will do that for you.

To illustrate, I'd like to share a personal experience that happened in our family. Debbie and the boys were sitting at the breakfast table one morning, and I was gone to a conference to speak. Debbie rubbed her arms with her hands and commented, "Brrr, I sure am cold." Trenton, our oldest son, quickly got up from the table, went upstairs, got Debbie a sweater, came down and held it for her to put on. First, he was thinking of Debbie's needs before his own. Second, he was being a gentleman by helping her. He held the sweater for mom to put on. She said, "Thank you so much, Trenton. I appreciate you getting the sweater for me. That is very thoughtful of you." He said, "I'm just trying to be like Dad." Those are powerful words coming from a child. (Trenton's response was humbling to me, but true.) Does that challenge this dad? Oh, yeah. Is this dad perfect? Far from it.

Do our kids want to be like us? It scares me to think my kids would be just like me in several areas in my life. There are none of us who are perfect. I want them to see a godly dad and a godly mom. We need to model a true Christian walk in front of them and be the real deal.

Intimate Conversation

The third lure we use to catch our spouse is...Intimate Conversation. This is what it took to "catch 'em:"

When you were first dating, you held nothing back and you talked about absolutely everything. If you thought about it, it came out. You verbalized your every thought. That was it. You didn't think whether or not you should share something. You trusted they wouldn't reject you or put you down. You felt safe. You made yourself totally vulnerable and put your whole self into the relationship. Can you remember back to that time? You shared absolutely everything on your mind and heart with your date.

Are you still willing to risk and be vulnerable? Why were you willing to risk in the first place with your spouse? Because, you felt safe and were willing to do whatever it took to win them over. Most guys, a few years into marriage, really don't see it as a "risk" issue. They would say they are just being lazy. But if you dig a little deeper, there is a fear and it may be the fear of making yourself vulnerable.

How has your conversation changed now? Do you still put yourself wholly into your relationship? Do you still share your intimate thoughts and dreams? Do you still make yourself vulnerable in your communication with your spouse? I pray and hope that you do. They need to be your best friend–the one you talk about everything with. Do you know what the average couple's communication has turned to now? Picture this...the husband comes home from work and the wife says, "Hey, honey, how was your day? His response is, "Fine." She says, "So, what did you do today?" He says, "Work." She says, "Who'd you see?" He says, "People." Is that intimate conversation? No. Now, I know some of you are thinking, "That was really weird, Joe. How did you know that's what goes on in our house?" Intimate conversation is focused conversation with intense talking and listening. Guys, I'm sorry, but this can't be done with the TV on. Some guys are real creative and think they've got this figured out. They say to their wives, "Hey honey, we can watch the show and talk during the commercials." Sorry, but it doesn't work.

God gave us two ears and one mouth so we need to do twice as much listening as we do talking. James 1:19 sums this up perfectly. "But everyone must be quick to hear, slow to speak and slow to anger." James 1:19 (NASB) We get it backwards from what God's Word says. We become quick to speak, slow to hear and then we're quick to anger. Then we wonder why things aren't working out. We need to do it God's way and God's order is always the best order.

From the studies that have been done studying the elements of communication, this is how they've been broken down:
- Non-Verbal–55%

- Tone–38%
- Words–7%

The bottom line is our body language and tone really reflect our demeanor and account for the largest part of the communication cycle. This doesn't discount our words, but shows how important all of these elements are. Your body language, tone and words mean EVERYTHING when communicating.

"Listening with your heart and truly understanding is one of the best gifts you can give your spouse! "

Most people admit that listening is one of the hardest parts when it comes to communication. Listening with your heart and truly understanding is one of the best gifts you can give your spouse! Debbie and I have been talking before, and then she'll pause, (and boy do I hate this pause). Here comes the dreaded question, "Tell me what I just said." I've analyzed this scenario and found I can generally have three responses when she says this to me.

The first response is to confess and say, "I don't have a clue. I wasn't listening very well. I don't know what you were trying to tell me. Would you please tell me again? I promise to listen better this time." If you don't know what your spouse is trying to tell you, don't try to make something up. Or, you can be real creative and say this, "Well, honey you said it so well, I don't think I can repeat it back as well as you said it." That one might help to lighten the moment a little bit. Here's the point in the first response. If you don't know, just be honest and say, "I don't know, I wasn't listening. If you'll tell me again, I'll listen."

The second response is, "I know what you told me, but I don't know what you told me". In other words, "I heard what you said, but I wasn't truly listening". It stayed in my brain just long enough for me to repeat it back like a good little parrot. It went in one ear and right out the other. I would be truthful and explain to her, "You said this, this and this," explaining specifics of the conversation. If she came back in five minutes and asked "What were we just talking about again?" I'd have to say, "Hmmmmmm, I don't know." I listened, but I didn't comprehend.

Here comes the third response. If I'm listening to what James 1:19 says, I can respond with, "Debbie, here's what you said, here's what it sounds like is going on, and here's how you feel about it." Do you see the difference? We need to work on not just listening, but comprehending what we're hearing too.

Do you still provide that safe environment for your spouse to share everything? Do you demean or put your spouse down for what they share? If our spouse feels demeaned or put down, it's as if they go into a shell. As time goes on like that, they will go further and further back into this shell until they feel it's no longer a safe environment for them to share their thoughts with you. They start shutting down. The more you put them down or make them feel stupid for having a thought, the less they will share with you. Sometimes the reason the communication has stopped in your relationship is not because your spouse won't talk to you, but because you have destroyed that safe environment for them to do so. Every time they try to talk, you're demeaning or putting them down. Every time you put them down, they go further back into their shell until eventually they won't come out anymore. They won't stick their neck out for anything! A wall is now built up between you and your spouse. Do you know how to get them out of that shell? First, apologize. Then you have to prove to them you mean it and that you are going to provide the safeness you once gave. The proof is in the actions!

What can happen in strong male leaders is they cut their wife off mid-sentence, and they control the conversation. They may not be demeaning, but it doesn't show respect or honor to their wife's input, directions or point of view.

"If you want to change what you're getting, change what you're giving." Chances are if you treat your wife like a queen, then she'll treat you like a king, or if you treat your husband like a king, then he'll treat you like a queen. Now, don't treat her like a queen just to be the 'king', but here's the point. YOU be the first one to make a move in your relationship. A lot of times husbands and wives come to a stalemate. It's when both parties say, "I'm not giving in or crossing that line." It's like the game tug-of-war. You are at one end of a rope and your spouse is at the other end. You're both pulling with all your might. It's as if that conflict has become a marital tug-of-war between spouses. What happens if someone stops pulling? The other stops also after they fall to the ground. If you would just drop the rope, your spouse would stop pulling in the opposite direction. Someone has to drop the rope first! This tug-of-war continues until both partners build up resentment, and it turns into a major problem that can split up a couple totally. It tears apart the emotional attachment that has glued you together. It takes one person to say, "If I want to change what I'm getting, I need to change what I'm giving." If you want to change what you're getting, don't wait on your spouse. You need to take the initiative, step up and change what you're giving. You'll end up getting different results for yourself.

Quality Time

The fourth lure we use is...Quality Time. This is what it took to "catch 'em":

You wanted to and did spend every waking hour with that special person. You couldn't get enough of them. Even when your dates were over, you would go home and call each other. The guy's conversation probably went something like this; "Hey babe...you sure looked fine tonight. What time can I pick you up in the morning? You know, I love you SO much! I don't think I can love you any more than I do right now or my heart will burst!" Now, I know some of you talked for hours on the phone. I had one couple at a conference who talked for 10 hours, long distance, internationally while they were dating. Their phone bill was $964 dollars. Ouch! It was cheaper to get married! The point is this, you couldn't get enough quality time with that special person before you were married. You longed to be together. You did activities together. You spent quality time together.

Here's what it takes to keep "em" when it comes to quality time: Make it a priority to spend time together. Have you stopped "dating" and making "quality time" for each other? Just because you're married, doesn't mean the word "date" has to leave your vocabulary. Courting means you're trying to "woo" them and win them over to your side. It is active dating with a specific goal in mind...to stay close and grow in your oneness. We have friends who arrange for a baby-sitter to come every one to two weeks so they can have a "date night" and spend quality together. You should look forward to those times when you can be together.

Dating takes some time, effort, and planning, but it is well worth the effort you put into it. Remember, once they're hooked, you have to keep reeling them in tenderly. You must make it a priority to spend quality time together. Your children's security is built upon the strength of your relationship as husband and wife. The husband and wife relationship is the core of the family. How strong is your family based upon this statement? What changes do you need to make?

> **"Your children's security is built upon the strength of your relationship as husband and wife."**

The best time to work on an issue, or problem, is when it's not an issue. I would venture to say there are some couples who purchased this book who feel they have a strong marriage and bought it in order to enrich their relationship. I'm glad you did! There may be others of you who feel you are in that "existing" phase of marriage; things aren't bad, but they aren't great either. Then there are still others of you who feel you are struggling. You don't like your spouse any more. It may be at this time, you are facing thoughts of a divorce. Perhaps, some of you have already talked to lawyers or are in the process of working on divorce papers. This book may be your last hope. You may be asking, "Can God do some great things in my marriage?" Oh yeah, but only if you let go of your pride and the hurt you're hanging on to. Let it go, and give it to God.

Please understand this, the best time to work on a problem isn't at 11:00 at night! This turns into what we call "intense moments of fellowship." It doesn't work, because you're both tired. Save some of your prime time to talk through and about specific areas in your marriage. Regardless of where you are in your marriage, the best time to work on an issue is when it's not an issue.

Let me explain this with an example. I had been in the corporate world of commercial finance before the Lord called me to full time ministry. I have experienced those times when the managers were pulled into the conference room, and we were told that we were about to lose one of our largest accounts. We were told our bonuses, and our profit margins were in jeopardy. What were we going to do? We were told we had to do something to keep the customer. Do you think the ideas came flowing freely at that point? Usually not, because everybody was in a panic. It was a meeting out of weakness with emotions on high.

I've also been in meetings where the managers were called in and we were told one of our largest customers had just signed a long-term commitment. They loved us. Things were going great and we wanted to make our relationship even better and stronger with this customer. We were asked, "What are some things we can do to make the relationship even stronger than it is?" Do you think ideas started coming out then? You'd better believe it! The ideas started flying because it was a meeting out of strength, not one out of fear or weakness.

Some of you are thinking, "My marriage is doing okay." Let me ask you, will you be bold enough to work on an area of your marriage when there isn't a problem? Will you decide right now to make a certain area stronger? When you make the proactive commitment to work on areas when they aren't heating up, then you can make huge strides in strengthening your marriage. At ten o'clock at night you are tired. It's the end of a long hard day. That isn't the time to strengthen those issues. That's when it turns into those "intense moments of fellowship" or conflict. Right now is the time when you can do that—when the issues aren't at the boiling point.

Here's another thought. If what you are doing now isn't working, go back to a time when it did work and do more of that. We do a lot of things in life that don't work, but we keep doing them out of habit or routine. If what you are doing now doesn't work, then stop! **A lot of people don't need to start with a "to-do" list, they need to start with a "stop doing" list.** We need to start focusing on what works and stop doing what doesn't work. We must make quality time for each other and not let the demands of life pull us apart.

Suppose you were to put your spiritual walk into a graph called "Your Salvation Zeal Meter." The day you accepted Christ (the most important day of your life) starts the graph in the upper left corner...the starting point. Would your line be increasing or decreasing? I believe the closest the average Christian has been in their relationship with the Lord is on the day they accepted Christ into their life. They've been falling away ever since. Their graph line is decreasing on the "Salvation Zeal Meter."

In comparison to that, consider doing the same thing for your marriage. Let's suppose you were to include a graph called "Marriage Zeal Meter." This represents the second most important day of your life, the day you married your spouse. I believe for the average marriage, the closest most couples have been to their spouse is their wedding day. Likewise, they've been falling away ever since.

What do you notice about these two areas when you compare them? They are pretty much the same, aren't they? They're going in the same direction. When your spiritual life is suffering, guess what happens to your marriage? It goes down also. When your marriage is suffering, guess what happens to your spiritual life? It goes down as well. When one of them is strong, guess what happens to the other one? The other one will be strong. That's why it's important to keep a good balance between these two areas. They go hand-in-hand. Hence, the importance of your personal daily time with the Lord and prayer with your spouse is a huge component to having a great marriage. This is what will help to strengthen your marriage. The closer you get to God, the closer you'll get to each other as represented in the triangle below.

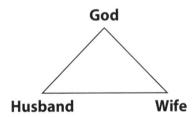

Here's a quote to live by. "If you keep doing what you're doing, you'll keep getting what you're getting. To get different results, something has to change." Another way to say it is, "More of the same will not bring about change." In other words, if you keep spending more money than you have coming in every month, you're going to keep going into debt. So, you have to make a change. It's the same with your marriage. Things won't change automatically. You must make changes to get different results! I pray you will make some changes to strengthen your marriage with the Lord's help.

Do you remember the lures we talked about? (Looks, Emotional Attachment, Intimate Conversation and Quality Time) These are the lures you used to "catch" your spouse, and it will be these lures that keep drawing you back to one another. What it takes to catch 'em, IS what it takes to keep 'em!

Application Time

What lure most attracted you to your spouse?

....
....
....
....

What specific lures need the most change?

....
....
....
....

What changes do you need to make to keep your spouse hooked on you?

....
....
....
....

Prayer Topic

Lord, I thank you so much for my spouse. Thank you for allowing me to spend my life with them. Help me to remember the basics in our marriage so we will stay fully in love for a lifetime!

Chapter 3

Marriage Busters

What makes you lose that spark in your marriage? What changes you from meeting your spouses' every need, want and desire? If I could help you determine five major reasons why couples have "bumps" in the road and then give you ways to strengthen each area, wouldn't you pay special attention to that? Of course you would. Here are some common hindrances to "bust" your marriage. We will call these areas "marriage busters." I will identify five "marriage busters" to you and then show you ways to keep them out of your marriage. Once you can recognize what the "buster" is, you can work on "keepin' em."

Marriage Buster #1 is...Your life and marriage become <u>commonplace</u> and <u>routine</u>

Are you caught up in a routine that never changes? Is your marriage on autopilot? Ladies, does this sound like your day? You wake up in the morning, you get yourself ready, you get the kids ready, you get breakfast ready, you get lunches ready, you take the kids to school, you do a few things around the house, you pick up the kids from school, you get supper ready, you clean up, you get some things ready for the next day, and then you fall into bed. This is a slow day without any special events to attend. The next day you do it all over again. It's the classic routine. You do the same things day in and day out. In marriage, we get stuck in routines and lose some of that zeal, freshness and excitement that we once had in our relationship. Our schedules rule us instead of us ruling our schedules.

There are two words in our vocabulary that we tend to forget in marriage. The first word is spontaneous and the second is creative. When I say spontaneous, what are some things that immediately come to your mind? Adventure, fun, leaving town, not planned, excitement, unexpected, going to Dairy Queen for supper and eating ice cream first (Yum). Spontaneous is spur of the moment, and we ALL need some of this in our marriage.

Now for some of you, planning something two weeks from now is majorly spontaneous. Your spouse might fall off their chair if you planned something that short in advance. Spontaneity means excitement and surprises. Every marriage needs this ingredient to keep it alive and exciting.

What are some things that come to your mind when I say the word creative? Planning, something that takes thought, new and surprising...a different way of doing something. Creative is something out of the norm, out of the ordinary. Being creative takes some thought. Is it easier to be spontaneous or creative? For most folks it's easier to be spontaneous. Being creative takes a little bit of work and time, but it's well worth it in the end.

One of my wife's main love languages is receiving gifts. She also has a stipulation with that, though. The gifts I give her have to be $5.00 or less. Wow! That forces me to be creative. She is very prudent. Would she rather me stop at a local grocery store and buy a bunch of flowers for $4.88 or stop and pick a bunch of flowers on the way home? She would rather me pick them, because it took some thought and because they're free.

Be romantic and surprise her. Take her places. Go on picnics, take walks together, go shopping or to a ball game together, go out on dates without the kids, plan a weekend get-away. Be creative. Women love romance and love the thoughtfulness you put into it. Don't get stuck in the rut of commonplace or in a routine with no adventures. Make it a point to keep things fresh, spontaneous and creative in your marriage.

Marriage Buster #2 is...Selfishness

Selfishness is the root of almost all marriage problems. In fact, when selfishness creeps in, it is at the root of almost any relationship problem we have. Any time "self" gets in the way, there will be a problem. I have never once talked or counseled with a couple in which one of the individuals has said, "It's all my fault. I'm the one who's not been meeting my spouse's needs. No blame belongs to them." What is said is more along the lines of, "You wouldn't believe what he or she is doing. They're not meeting my needs." These individuals are quick to point their fingers at their spouses instead of looking at themselves. They don't stop and realize there are areas they need to improve in too. If we can rid ourselves of our "self" problem, we can get rid of the majority of our problems.

I believe the root of selfishness is pride. There is a spiritual implication here as pride is sin. Selfishness is about our exaltation and not about God's exaltation. As we release the pride in our own lives by submitting to God, our attitudes and demeanors will be radically changed for our families.

Remember the example we looked at in Ephesians 5? Jesus was more concerned about others than himself. He came to serve...not to be served. The Christian life is about others, not about us. In order for Christ to live in and through us, we have to die to ourselves. That's what needs to be applied when selfishness is an issue. We need to put the needs of our spouse before our own. Who are you more concerned about, yourself or your spouse? Our attitude should be that of Christ. Philippians 2:3-5 says: "Do nothing from selfishness or empty conceit, but with humility of mind regard one another as more important than yourselves; do not merely look out for your own personal interests, but also for the interests of others. Have this attitude in yourselves which was also in Christ Jesus." (NASB) We are commanded to have this attitude. It's not a request. It's a command.

Marriage Buster #3 is...<u>Children</u>

A fact of life is that your time is divided when you have children. When you have a little one, the time you once had alone as husband and wife is greatly reduced. Children are a joy, but they are a lot of work. If you're not an organizer, a self-motivator and a hard worker, your life gets put into the "survival mode." Chaos rules in your house, and you lose that focus you once had for your spouse.

"Parents get so focused on their kids they forget about each other!"

It's easy for our lives to be centered around our kids. We dearly love our children, but practically speaking children can be a marriage buster! This is why...Children can become the center of the family instead of an addition to the family. Parents get so focused on their kids they forget about each other! So many families put the kids first while they are growing up. Everything is centered around them. It is as if you have put your lives on hold to do everything your child wants to do.

We, as parents, want to give them everything that we had or didn't have when we were growing up. If our kids say they really want something, then mom and dad truly want to oblige them. If we give them everything they want, we are actually teaching them to be selfish and spoiled. In teaching our kids to be selfish, we are actually setting them up for failure in marriage. If everything revolves around them when they are kids, and they get everything they want, then they will expect everything in their marriage to revolve around them as well.

Studies show that the two most stressful times in a marriage are when the first child is born and when the last child leaves. Now, I'm going to do some stereotyping, but the following scenario is common in counselors' and pastors' offices everyday all over the country. Listen to this...When the first child is born, the wife will do what she knows best. Her natural instincts kick in. She will pour all of her time, attention and energy into taking care of her child. The husband at this time may feel a little bit alienated, because once he had all of her attention, and now he feels a little separated from his wife. This is a difficult adjustment time for most men. As a result, a man may start working more, or take up a new hobby to fill up his 'extra' time. He will start doing new things to take up the time that he had been spending with his wife. In essence, the wife is having an affair with her child, and the husband is having an affair with his work or hobbies. For this couple, the emotional attachment that attracted them to each other and has held them together, has now become detached. In essence you start living separate lives. That's a dangerous place to be, because one of them might possibly get "hooked" by someone else while they're out there floating around not attached to their spouse.

That same marriage continues to deteriorate over a period of 20 to 25 years. When the last child gets ready to leave, the wife's emotional attachment goes where? It walks right out the door with that child. Many times, the wife will go back to her husband and suggest they spend more time together, travel, and do other things to fill her empty time. The husband often responds that he felt abandoned several years before. He's happy where he is right now, and he doesn't want to change or change his schedule. This husband and wife have become roommates who live under the same roof.

When the kids are gone, they realize they've been married for the kids. One day they wake up and ask, "Who in the world is this person who's been sleeping in bed with me? I don't know who they are. I know their name, but I don't really know this person." They haven't spent time working on their relationship. This couple's focus has been more on parenting than on partnering. The partnering aspect between a husband and wife is the glue of the family. A family is only as strong as the husband/wife relationship.

> *"The partnering aspect between a husband and wife is the glue of the family. A family is only as strong as the husband/wife relationship."*

This scenario is a common reason why so many couples married 25 to 35 years get divorced. If you look back at a lot of these couples' situations, I believe you'd see that their last child was getting ready to leave, had just left, or had left in the last couple of years. They woke up one day and realized they didn't really know the person they were sleeping with. There was no reason for that couple to stay together in their eyes. They had been staying together merely for the kids. They've been roommates living in the same house. That's a sobering thought.

The first couple, in the scenario above, is still getting their act together, and the last couple forgot what their act was supposed to be. Many couples can relate to this troubling scenario. They wonder what they can do about it or if it's too late for them. Well, let me tell you…It's never too late to work on your relationship and make it the way it should be! To realize areas of improvement, a couple must stay focused on the partnering aspect of their marriage relationship.

On a side note, many couples truly enjoy the empty nest time, although there are some changes which come along with this transition. These are the couples who have made an investment in their marriage and haven't just stayed together because of the kids.

Before we move on to the next marriage buster, here are a few tips on how to rule over chaos in your home:

Wake up each day like you're on a mission with a list in hand. If you aim at nothing, then you'll hit it every time! Make a list for the day of everything you need to do. If you don't plan your schedule, someone else will plan it for you. Prioritize the items on your list by importance. You must be organized, or you will become exasperated with yourself, your kids and your spouse.

Before the Lord called me into full-time ministry, I worked in the corporate world in commercial finance for 10 years. Now, I know what it's like to be real busy. I know what it's like to have several people needing you all of the time and not being able to return calls fast enough. The last position I had was Area Manager for a fortune 500 company for 19 states in the Eastern U.S. I know busy! I'm going to share with you one question which helped me more than anything in prioritizing. "What is the most important thing I need to be doing right now?" Whatever it is...do it! Don't put it off, and don't procrastinate. If it's number one on your radar screen, no matter how hard it is...do it! After you get that done, then what question should you ask yourself? "What is the most important thing I need to be doing now?" This helps me to prioritize by order of importance, and I believe it will help you as well.

- Start on #1 of your list, and don't go on to #2 until #1 is completed. Stay focused on your list all day. Don't allow yourself to get sidetracked. If you don't do the things that are the most important, you will end the day feeling defeated, frustrated and possibly blaming others for not getting things done.

- Stay FOCUSED all day on your list. Your list cannot get completed with you on the phone. Be smart with what you choose to do with your time. Stay balanced if more important things come up than what is on your list.

- Work hard at home to free your time up when your spouse gets home for family time. Debbie took this time on as her "job" by taking care of our home during work hours so we could maximize family time at night. She would make sure the house stayed clean and her other responsibilities stayed current. This means baths were

CHAPTER 3: MARRIAGE BUSTERS

done for the kids too. This is not saying she never allowed herself some fun time or time to just spend with the boys. She made it her motto to work first then play second. This is something she took on by herself. She was never told by me "cracking the whip" or anyone else to do this.

- **"Clock out"** when your spouse gets home or when you get home from work. This doesn't mean you have a time clock hanging on the wall. This is a mental state of being. This is a transition time from work time to family time. **Family time** is just that. It may be playing games, watching TV together; it may be conversation around the table. It could be any number of things, but it definitely needs to be quality time spent together as a family.

Couple Time:

The core of the family is the husband and wife relationship. As this relationship goes, so goes the rest of the family. "Couple Time" is a model to help you focus on your relationship as husband and wife. Let me ask you a pointed question. Have you focused so much on parenting that you've forgotten about partnering with your spouse? That is the reason for couple time. I have the opportunity to travel around the country and conduct the "Hooked For Life" marriage enrichment events. I actually get the most feedback on the practicality of the couple time. It's simple and it works! Here it is:

There are three basic ingredients for couple time:

1. **Clock Out** — When I get home from work, Debbie and I both "clock out" mentally from work time and transition to family time. You must learn to clock out at home. If you don't, your frustration will come out and flow onto your family.

2. **Family Time** — Next, we have family time which is simply a time to focus on our family, spend time together, bond as a family and do fun things together. Have baths done, dinner ready (or almost ready), so you can spend the evening together as a family. Family time should be your ultimate goal each day! If you don't have that all important family time, families crumble and spouses drift apart! Love is spelled T-I-M-E!

3. **Couple Time** — Lastly, we have couple time. This is an un-interrupted time for Debbie and I to spend quality time together.

Here's a few more helps to maximize your couple time:
If you have small children, put them to bed early so you can have "couple time." During the school year, our boys go to bed between 7:30 and 8:00. Now, I can hear you groaning and wailing, "Joe, our kids will NEVER go to bed that early! What do you do, give your kids a horse tranquilizer?" Our boys stay very healthy because they get enough sleep. They NEED this sleep. With the kids in bed, you don't have to hire a babysitter and can have a date at home. It doesn't have to cost a thing. You can play games, have a bowl of ice cream, talk, and just spend quality time together. After they're in bed, it's party time for Debbie and me! If your children are older and 9:30 bed time is not an option, you have to be creative to find other ways to have quality couple time together. Maybe let the kids have some room time to play or read while you talk. Here's another idea I suggest: Tell them that mom and dad learned about this thing called "Couple Time," and from 8:00 to 8:30 tonight you would like private time in your room. I would suggest for you to leave your door open at first, so they can see you are just spending time together and they don't feel threatened. They aren't to come in or interrupt you unless it involves fire or blood! Be ready, because they will test you. They're going to be wondering what in the world are mom and dad doing and is everything ok. Assure them ahead of time that all is well, and mom and dad want and need to talk regularly to keep their relationship strong. Couple time allows us to have time together to have fun, work on a project, talk or whatever. If you don't plan time for each other it won't happen automatically. The fact of the matter is... What's planned and prioritized gets done, bottom line.

"If you don't plan time for each other it won't happen automatically."

I don't believe the average couple gets even five minutes a night of quality time together or time to talk. If you make this a priority it can revolutionize your marriage and family! Create "couple time" at night instead of "chore time." If you are always having chore time or TV time, you will never have couple time! You need time at night with just the two of you. Maybe start having regular date nights. You must continue to focus on each other and not just on the kids. Remember, you are showing your kids an example of what marriage is, and their marriage will be a lot like yours due to your influence. Would you want your kids to have the same kind of marriage you have? If not, what changes do you need to make? Your kids will feel secure when they see your deep love for each other!

This time of uninterrupted communication and focusing is much needed in any marriage. With the TV off and children taken care of, you as husband and wife can have quality time together. Remember, this is one of the hooks that attracted you to your spouse, so it's critical to have this 'connecting' time in your marriage. Give each other quality time...not left-over time. Enjoy your couple time! We sure do!

Marriage Buster #4 is... Activities

Are you balanced in all of your family's activities? Do you have SO many activities that your head is swimming? Do you have more nights during the week that have activities than nights that don't? Some of your activities may include church activities, school activities, work activities, husband's recreational activities, wife's social activities, and the biggie is this...kids' ball games.

Let's park right here for a little bit. I know many parents who feel the need to have each child competing in every sport. First we have soccer, then baseball, then summer camps, then football, then basketball. Most of these sports start before the prior one ends and you have to double up on games and practices. Where do we draw the line? Where is the fun family time? You say, "Oh, but I want my kids to have a chance for college scholarships and to make the big league." What about games or practices on Sunday or Wednesday night? When you allow your kids to miss church for a ball game or practice, what are your actions saying to them? You are saying that the game or practice is more important than God. Actions speak so much louder than any words you could ever speak. I've talked to the leaders who plan these games and practices on Sunday and Wednesday nights. They say that if parents were to say no to it, they would change it; but they've never had a problem with it from parents. All it would take is for you to take a stand. Yes, your child might miss that opportunity, but what is more important to you and them in the long run?

Are you and your family going in all different directions at all different times? You may need to make drastic changes in the amount of activities in which you are involved. Time with your spouse and family should come first, and everything else can be put on hold. You may even need to eliminate all activities, so you can have time to get back to the basics in your marriage and family. The bottom line is this...What's more important to you, your activities or your marriage? I pray it's your marriage.

"I really believe that busyness is the number one thing tearing families apart."

I frequently have pastors and many people ask me this question: "Joe, what do you believe is the biggest thing tearing families apart today?" That's an easy question for me. **I really believe that busyness is the number one thing tearing families apart.** Families are SO busy they don't have time to be a family. Activities have become more of a priority than time together. Your kids don't really want things or something more to do...they want you!

There are parents who are so busy with gymnastics one night, baseball the next and soccer the next evening; it goes on and on. Parents are so busy "going" and "doing," family time consists of going through the drive through at a fast food restaurant and eating in the car together on the way to the next activity. These parents may be spending time with their kids, but it's not quality time. The key is that you must maintain a balance in which activities your family participates, so you can have fun and quality time as a family. **You know, there's a difference between scheduling and prioritizing. You can schedule things and be organized, but your priorities may still be way out of line. Your schedule may be filled with "good" things, but where is the room for the "best" things?** Take a look at your main priorities first and then make your schedule based on your priorities. I believe this can change your whole perspective on busyness. We must learn to prioritize our lives! Mom and dad, let me ask you this question: When was the last time you spent 15 minutes with your children just looking into their eyes, getting into their world, and not being distracted by the TV, a newspaper, or the hurriedness to get to another activity? If you don't have time to do this on a regular basis, then you're too busy. What's more important to you, your activities or your marriage and family? Remember, they don't want things, they want you!

Marriage Buster #5 is...No Animal Attraction

Have you lost your touch or passion for each other? Do you remember some of the strong sexual urges you once had when you were first married? This magnetism was so strong because it was new and because you really knew each other. You were intimate in everything , not just sexually. Do you remember the first time you were sitting together, and your arms touched? Man, you could just feel the energy pulsating through you. What about the non-sexual touches...likd holding your spouse's hand, putting your arm around your spouse's waist, sneaking your arm around their shoulders. These little 'touches' create that animal attraction, that spark and zeal between you as husband and wife. When you become distracted with any of the marriage busters, your physical relationship suffers too. This "animal attraction" is the strongest when you feel loved and are emotionally close to your spouse!

Application Time

What do you like most about "Couple Time" and how can you start it in
your home?

. . . .
. . . .
. . . .
. . . .

What marriage buster is most prevalent in your marriage?

. . . .
. . . .
. . . .
. . . .

What changes do you need to make to keep the marriage busters
out of your relationship?

. . . .
. . . .
. . . .
. . . .

Prayer Topic

Lord, thank you for giving us to each other. Help us to see the areas in
our marriage where things could negatively pull against us. Help us to not
become so busy that we forget each other and you.

Chapter 4

What If They Get Off The Hook?

We've looked at ways you hooked your spouse, ways to catch 'em, and ways to keep 'em. We've looked at some marriage busters that can creep into a marriage and can create division between a husband and wife that can seriously hurt your marriage. Let me ask you this...If you don't do these things to "keep 'em" and the marriage busters are prevalent in your marriage, what could happen next? Your marriage would just exist or the love would be gone. One of the more devastating things that can happen is an affair.

This can crush and destroy a marriage and family. Oh, how this hurts so many! You think it is only hurtful to that couple. How wrong that is! It affects not only the husband and wife, but the children, immediate family, extended family, friends, church members, co-workers, and the same for the other person in the affair.

The Bible calls an affair adultery. The three main classes of affairs in the Bible, according to Dave Carder in his book, _Torn Asunder,_ are:

Class I — This is a one night stand. David & Bathsheba are the examples here.

Class II — The affair is gradual and an emotional connection. An example is Samson and Delilah.

Class III — Affairs due to sexual addictions. (Multiple partners) An example is Eli's sons.

This is a serious issue for our society today. The church is not immune from affairs. It's something that is permeating our society and our churches. It's not a fun thing to write about, but it needs to be discussed. According to Peggy Vaughan (Author of "The Monogamy Myth," first published in 1989 by Newmarket Press and third edition published 2003) **conservative infidelity statistics estimate 60% of men and 40% of women will have an extramarital affair.** Other reports suggest an astounding 50-65% of husbands and 45-55% of wives will have extramarital affairs by the time they are forty years old.[1] That blows me away! This issue is crippling our society and our churches today. It is so damaging to a relationship. The tsunami of infidelity not only affects your marriage, but your extended family, your work, church, friendships and more. Instead of working on the relationship they're in, they think it is easier to look for a new or better relationship. Ideas like this are as far from the truth as you can get. If you leave or escape from your current relationship to get away from the problems, you're kidding yourself, because you are part of the problem. You end up taking your problems with you if they're not worked through, plus you pick up additional baggage in the process.

I'm sure you've heard the expression, "The grass is greener on the other side." Here are some variations to this cliché in regards to this topic of infidelity:

1. The grass is greenest where you water it and take care of it.
2. The grass on the other side has to be cut just like the grass on your side.
3. Plus, it's someone else's grass.

You must keep your guard up! If you don't have your guard up, you leave yourself unprotected.

In the upcoming chapters I am going to be covering some basic needs for the husband and wife and let you rank them according to the importance you put on them. This personalizes it for you. You may ask, "If I do all of the list for my spouse, will that guarantee they won't get off the hook?" No. What does it take? It takes a daily effort of tenderly reeling them in. It is in those little things you do for your spouse every day to let them know they are important and valued. But as you'll discover in the coming chapters, it really does help to know their specific needs.

Do you remember the example I gave you about the wet bar of soap. What happens if you hold a bar of soap too tightly? It goes sailing through the air, doesn't it? It slips right out of your hands. What happens if you hold that same bar of soap too loosely? It slips right out of your hands to the floor. You have to hold it tenderly or it will get away from you. It is the same with your marriage. You need the right balance to keep your spouse. If you hold on too tightly, you suck the life out of them. On the other hand if you hold them too loosely, they will slip away from you.

It takes the right balance to keep your spouse close to you.

When an affair has been committed, it affects the husband and wife differently. If the wife has been unfaithful, the first thing the husband thinks about and is going to dwell on is the physical aspect. Any information he receives goes into his mind which becomes a video player. He'll play the information, like it's a video, in his mind over and over thousands of times. Any new information he receives will be added to that tape as he continues playing it over and over in his mind. He thinks about the physical aspects first because his wife is his "property," so to speak, when it comes to the physical area of his marriage. He feels violated since this area is so important to him. The second thing the husband thinks about is that the trust is broken.

If the husband has been unfaithful, the first thing the wife thinks about is the trust being broken. If the husband comes home ten minutes late, the thought of the affair comes into her mind. The wife may ask questions such as: "Where were you? Why were you late? Who were you talking to? Who was at work? Who did you talk to on the cell phone on the way home?"

Why is she asking all those questions? The trust has been broken between them. The husband's words and promises mean very little to her

"Forgiveness is an event and trust is the process built from that event."

now. Can trust be rebuilt? It can, but it takes time. It's a process. Forgiveness is a process. Forgiveness is an event and trust is the process built from that event. You can ask forgiveness and grant forgiveness, but trust has to be built over time. It doesn't happen overnight, but it starts the process of reconciliation. This can be accomplished as the husband and wife mutually submit to each other and put the needs of their spouse first.

An affair usually happens because both participants are living away from the Lord and because they are both living in the "selfish mode." The person who has committed the affair is desperately searching for love, appreciation, affection, acceptance and to be valued. If you don't meet the needs of your spouse, it may cause them to stray and become emotionally attached to someone else. You may say, "Now wait a minute, Joe. I did everything I knew to do, and they still got off the hook." My response is that it takes two to tango. There are specific reasons why this person was looking elsewhere and why their lover may have filled a void they had. Meeting your spouse's specific needs is a practical way to strengthen your marriage. Later in the book I'll be sharing with the men on how to be "The Irresistible Husband" by meeting the nine basic needs of his wife. Then I'll be sharing with the women on how to be "The Irresistible Wife" by meeting the seven basic needs of her husband. You may say, "Joe, are you saying that if I do all nine of these for my wife or do all seven for my husband, they won't get off the hook?" I can't guarantee that, because when sin creeps into someone's life, any of us are capable of doing anything. You may have heard the expression, "Sin will take you further than you want to go, cost you more than you want to pay and keep you longer than you want to stay." No one makes a person have an affair. The individual has decided to make that wrong choice all by himself/herself.

What is lacking in someone's marriage is usually what draws them into an affair. It takes two people to get to the point of the affair, and I don't mean just the two people who are involved in the affair. The person who was unfaithful usually takes the brunt of the blame. It is true the unfaithful person made the choice to be unfaithful, but there was usually a reason why that person was looking to someone else to meet their needs. There was something lacking in their marriage. So, it's not right to throw all of the judgment on just one person who was unfaithful, it takes two to get to that point. Researchers have found that a majority of the time, an affair didn't start off being sexual — it was emotional.

"Whatever needs are being met in the affair are usually the same needs that are being neglected in the marriage.

If I were to ask an unfaithful spouse what it was that drew them into an affair, that person would say something like this: "I felt valued and appreciated. This person actually listened to me". If I asked that same person what was lacking in their marriage, they would respond by saying, "I did not feel valued by my spouse. My spouse never listened to me. When they did have something to say, it was always negative." Whatever needs are being met in the affair are usually the same needs that are being neglected in the marriage.

An affair is a feeling of value and acceptance. We desperately yearn and long to know we are valuable to our spouse! Anyone can place a gnawing need of feeling valued and accepted on the back burner, but it will eventually come out. This doesn't excuse the actions of the unfaithful spouse, but it does show some of the reasons why they may have gone in that direction.

So what sparks an affair?

Emotional attachment—not being cared for at home!

Intimate conversation—this person actually listens to me!

Quality time and praise—you are valuable to me! Another word that sums up this point is affirmation. Most affairs are affirming the other person and building them up by spending quality time with them and heaping on the praise.

Do you recognize these three areas? These are three of the four lures discussed in the first part of this book used to catch your spouse and then to keep 'em. An affair is the process of falling in love all over again, but for the wrong reasons. By letting these three lures go by the wayside, the emotional attachment between the spouses is being separated. This is a dangerous place to be because you could get "hooked" by someone else. **An affair is the start of the process of getting "hooked" like you were "hooked" with your spouse.** This other person dominates your thoughts. If your focus had stayed on your spouse, then you wouldn't be looking to fill your thoughts with anyone else!

Specific Warning Signs That Can Lead to Infidelity

This is not an all-inclusive list. If you recognize any of these or other things going on in your marriage, I hope the Holy Spirit will help you to realize that something is not right and you need to do something about it.

Here are a few specific warning signs which can lead to infidelity:

1. Having problems in your marriage and not seeking help. (In other words, you are just going through the motions.)
2. Feeling "trapped," or stuck in a routine with no feeling or romance.
3. A continual lack of sexual pleasure in your marriage.

4. Not feeling valued or appreciated by your spouse.
5. Having an "It can't happen to me" attitude. If you say, Joe, "I'm the last one who would ever have an affair!" Watch out...studies show the people who are 'unguarded' fall first.
6. Having uncommunicated or unrealistic expectations of your spouse.
7. Inventing excuses to visit someone of the opposite sex.
8. Increasing male/female contacts in normal environments. (For example—work, choir, recreational activities, etc...)
9. Being preoccupied with thoughts about another person. If you're having thoughts about someone else like, "If I were just married to him or her, I'd have it made." Be careful...your thoughts and emotions may be moving to someone else.
10. Exchanging gifts with a "friend" of the opposite sex.
11. Making daily/weekly contact with someone of the opposite sex by phone.
12. Putting yourself in situations where a "friend or coworker" might become more than that. One study found that 73% of men and 42% of women who had extramarital affairs met their partner at work. Let me camp out on this point for a while. I'd like to give you the following common scenario that is a typical way an affair can start in the work place...Here it is:

A guy goes down to the break room to fill up his coffee cup, and while he's there he notices a young lady filling up her water bottle. He doesn't recognize her so he asks her, "Are you new here?" She says she is and this is her first day. He wants to be polite, so he says, "Welcome to the team. If I can help you out in any way, just let me know." As she leaves he wants to be nice to her, so he adds, "I really like that dress you're wearing." She thanks him and walks out. Little does he know she is running on fumes in her marriage, and she starts to think, "My husband hasn't complimented me in a long time. He sure is a nice guy." The next day the same man goes to the break room again to fill up his coffee cup. Guess who happens to be there? You guessed it, that same young lady. He asked her how her first day was, and she says, "It was great. Everyone around here is so nice." He gets ready to leave, and she says to him, "By the way, I like that tie you are wearing today." He thanks her, and as he leaves he thinks, "That was awfully nice of her to compliment me. My wife hasn't complimented me in a long time. Boy, that young lady is pretty." After a couple of days like this, he notices she goes to fill up her water bottle around 10:00. Guess where he plans to be at 10:00 every morning? This goes on for a couple of weeks, and before you know it, both the man and the lady are finding ways to get to the break room to see the other person who is so nice and appealing to them. That is the stuff that affairs are made out of! Remember, most affairs don't start out as sexual things; they start out as emotional things where someone else is meeting the needs that are lacking in a marriage. You may ask, "Joe, why is the workplace so dangerous for marriages?" Think about this... People at the workplace look good, don't they? People dress for success. They dress for the next promotion they are trying to get. Also, when you work with some-one on projects, it builds a comradery and attachment. When you're working on these projects, you are talking freely about the pros and cons and how to make it work. You are working as a team. We spend most of our waking hours at work. Think about these characteris-tics: 1. Looks, 2. Emotional Attachment, 3. Intimate Conversation, 4. Quality Time. Do they sound familiar? All four are hooks we used to catch our spouse and are the ingredients in the above workplace sce-nario. These four ingredients are why the work area is such a breed-ing ground for affairs. Now, I know that some of you will be nervous and won't go to the break room at all now or will cover your eyes when a man or woman comes around you at work. You'll be saying, "Oh no, here comes a man/woman. Hurry and run the other way." I'm not trying to make you paranoid, but I hope you remember this example. I pray you'll guard yourself! We can't walk around with blinders on our eyes like horses, but we can have spiritual blind-ers as we ask God to help us protect our eyes, thoughts, bodies and lives. I pray you'll want to guard your life and your marriage!

13. Having to touch, embrace or glance at a particular person of the opposite sex.

14. Spending time alone with someone in particular of the opposite sex.

Let me ask you these questions: Are you in any of the above categories? Are you anywhere close? Did the Holy Spirit prick your heart while you were reading these? Did He convict you in another area not mentioned here? If so, get out now, and run as fast as you can and as far as you can. You may not see the danger and destruction coming, but an affair will tear your family apart!

Our oldest son took a karate class when we lived in Georgia. He had a great teacher, Chris Newbury. Chris was making a point one day…He said, "Your feet are your best defense." Now, I thought he was going to show them some special kick—like the 'crane' kick in the Karate Kid movie, but he wasn't done. This was his whole statement. "Your feet are your best defense…use them for running!" Wow! That was totally different than what I thought was coming. He explained to them if your attacker is on one side of the room, the door on the other side and you are in the middle, run for the door. If there is a way of escape, take it. Run for all you're worth. Don't fight unless you have to defend yourself. I hope you get the point of this…your feet are your best defense in staying out of an affair… use them for running! You have a way of escape by turning and running. Run away from the relationship that is luring you away from your spouse and stay faithful to your marriage vows. Take the exit…run from evil.

Proverbs 27:7 says this, "He who is full loathes honey, but to the hungry even what is bitter tastes sweet." (NIV) To the hungry person in their marriage, something bitter (like an affair) may taste sweet, but it is ultimately bitter in the end.

Do you feel resentment towards your spouse for giving up on your dreams and plans? Guys, has your wife given up on her desires to fulfill only yours? Wives, has your husband given up on his desires to fulfill only yours? A relationship takes two people going in the same direction. I've heard it put this way, "If I give up on myself, there is no 'us' anymore."

The person who is pulled into an affair feels like they are in a state of helplessness in their marriage. They see hope in someone else. An affair seems like true love, but that person is so blinded they can't see the danger and destruction coming if they give in to that affair.

The devil constantly has hooks out there for us. Have you ever caught a fish and the hook snagged them somewhere other than in their mouth?

Many people have. Maybe you caught it in the side, or the eye, or the tail. That fish was minding it's own business, enjoying life, just swimming along and then...WHAM...you hooked it. It wasn't looking for it at all! There are many lures and distractions out there that could snag us this way in this area of infidelity. You may be swimming along in your life and then...WHAM...you're caught. Here's the bottom line...You must be guarded and protected in these areas. If you aren't being proactive or choosing hedges or precautions ahead of time to know what's going on around you, you may get caught.

One hedge or precaution I have set up in advance in my life is not going out to eat with another woman by myself. You may say, "Joe, aren't you a little old-fashioned?" I don't believe I am at all. Let's say a lady called me, and she is trying to work things out with her husband. She asked me to meet her for lunch to discuss her problem. We meet for lunch at a local restaurant, and the table we are seated at is in the back corner. I'm innocently helping her. Little do I know another couple from church comes in to eat lunch together, and they see me in the back corner eating lunch with another woman who is not my wife. They will ask themselves things like, "Why is Joe with another woman? I wonder how he and Debbie are doing? You know, I haven't seen them together in a while." I don't want to be a stumbling block to someone else, but also...I don't trust myself. I have chosen in advance to make this a hedge in my life. If this situation comes up, my answer is already decided. I know men and women take business clients out to lunch, but it feels and looks awkward. Here's an answer I give when I'm asked to go out to eat or drive somewhere with another lady alone: "Thank you for the invitation. Is there someone else who could come along? It feels weird to be alone with someone without my wife there." That's a polite way to handle that situation. If that person says no, and is always trying to get you alone out by yourself...RUN...you may not be trying to start anything, but they might be!

Steve Green has a song titled "Guard Your Heart." It goes right along with what I've been writing about—keeping your marriage pure and choosing in advance how to react. Another favorite singing group of mine, Casting Crowns, has a song titled, "Slow Fade" which tells a similar story and gives the same warning. I encourage you to check out both of these songs and let the Lord speak to you while you listen.

Here are some specific hedges I've put in place to guard my heart:
1. Daily Devotions — Reading my Bible and having my prayer time.
2. Focus on my Marriage — Continually strengthen the relationship with my wife.
3. Time with my Family — Make them a priority with my scheduling.
4. Don't Ride Alone — Not riding alone with someone of the opposite sex unless they are a family member.
5. Don't Eat Alone — Not eating alone with someone of the opposite sex unless they are a family member.
6. Stay Away — Stay away from potential places or situations where you'd be alone with someone of the opposite sex.

I pray you'll want to guard your heart in advance to protect your life and your marriage. I'd like to ask you to have a special time together as husband and wife to commit together in this area to guard your hearts. Pray right now at home or where ever you are. Ask God to guard your eyes, your thoughts, your mind, and your desires. Ask Him to help your desires to be for your spouse only and to give you spiritual blinders. Ask Him to help your marriage grow stronger and be protected for His honor and glory!

As this chapter closes, let me explain another way you can be "hooked." Picture a fishing pole in front of you. Now, I'm going to stretch this example, but work with me, ok? The pole symbolizes God the Father; the line symbolizes Jesus Christ; and the lure symbolizes the Holy Spirit. They are all three working together to hook you. Are you feeling the tug on your heart? Is the Holy Spirit trying to reel you in? He is trying to hook you to become one of His prized trophies. Have you ever had a specific time and place when you asked Jesus to come into your heart and life? Give Him your heart and life today!

For more information go to one of these:

- www.billygraham.org (Click on "Spiritual Growth" at the top and How to Know Jesus in the drop down box)
- 1-888-NEED-HIM

Notes

1. Grant L. Martin, "Relationship, Romance, and Sexual Addiction in Extramarital Affairs," Journal of Psychology and Christianity 8, no. 4 (Winter 1989): 5.

Application Time

What does your spouse do that makes you feel most valued?

. . . .
. . . .
. . . .
. . . .

Plan your next "real" date.

. . . .
. . . .
. . . .
. . . .

What other changes do you need to make to keep your spouse hooked on you?

. . . .
. . . .
. . . .
. . . .

Prayer Topic

Lord, help me to keep my desires for my spouse only, so we may please You with our marriage. I pray I will show my spouse how valuable they are to me!

PART TWO

THE IRRESISTIBLE HUSBAND

HOW TO MEET THE NINE BASIC NEEDS OF YOUR WIFE

Irresistible...WOW! I love that word! When you hear the word "irresistible" what comes to your mind? Irresistible to me, means you are so drawn to something that you can't stay away from it. For some people, this could mean a candy bar or a favorite dessert. If you're not irresistible, then you're the opposite...resistible. Who's in control of making you irresistible to your spouse? You are. You can work on making yourself irresistible to your spouse by meeting some specific needs.

At the end of each section, both husbands and wives will have an opportunity to rank these needs or links in order of importance to you; one being the most important and nine being the least. Here's a point to remember, though. Just because something is ranked last on your spouse's list, it can't be neglected. It sure is nice to know what makes your spouse tick, but you must remember to help strengthen all of these areas.

Remember...you'll be ranking these after this section and then discussing them with your spouse. I won't be covering these in any particular order, but remember at the end of this chapter you ladies will get to rank these specific needs 1 to 9 in order of importance to you. This will customize needs for each one of you.

Guys, have you ever wanted a blueprint to know what makes your wife tick? You're getting ready to get it!

Chapter 5

Be A Spiritual Leader

In my opinion, most women are, initially, the spiritual leaders of their home. It is not because they necessarily want to be, but because their husbands aren't, so they feel they have to be. This is one of the hardest areas for most men. When you lead your family in spiritual matters, your wife will immediately put you on a whole different level of respect. Everything rises and falls on your leadership. It's up to you. It's up to you to get the family together to have devotions. Your wife needs you to take the lead in having devotions with the entire family. We usually have our family devotions time in the morning when we're eating breakfast, because it's a great way to start the day by putting God's Word and practical principles in our hearts and minds. Find a time that works for you...don't be afraid to try different times, but the key is to stick with it. This time is in addition to your own personal time you have alone with God. A resource for family devotions that I highly recommend is "Keys for Kids." They are simple, they work, and we personally get fed by them too. It is the absolute best resource for children's' devotionals I have come across. Their website is www.cbhministries.org, so check it out sometime.

A lot of guys ask me how they should start their personal devotions. Here's an average Joe's guide on how to start:

- **Read the Bible daily in Proverbs and Matthew.** There are 31 chapters in Proverbs — read one chapter a day for each day of the month. Whatever day of the month it is, that's the chapter you'll read. Also start in Matthew with one chapter a day. If you only manage a total of five verses a day, that's a great start and better than doing nothing. Ask the Lord to teach you and show you what He would have you do based on those few verses. How you can personally apply it to your life? Remember, start out with one chapter a day and build on that. Some of you may say, "Joe, I'm starting out with 10 chapters a day, and I'm going to stick with it. I want to do so much more." If you try to tackle too much, you may get discouraged. Think about this...How many people go to the gym after the first of each year with their New Year's resolutions firmly in hand? They go in with great intentions of getting in shape. They work out hard and then can barely move to get out of bed the next several days. They get discouraged and don't go back. The point is this...Start out slow, and grow as the Lord gives you strength and more of an appetite for Him. Remember, it's better to do five sit-ups a day than none.

- **Prayer Time.** I will share with you my personal prayer time format for you to consider as a guideline. The first part of my prayer time is **confession and forgiveness.** That's the time to get things right between the Lord and myself, and get the pipeline clear. I ask the Lord to search deep down in my heart and find anything that needs to be cleaned up. I will ask questions like, "Have I treated anyone badly? Did I respond wrong at any time? Was I short with my wife or kids? Am I growing weak in an area in my life?" It is a time to ask the Lord to search your heart and motives. It is a time of honest openness to the Lord and then a willingness to be cleansed by his forgiveness and mercy. Don't forget to get things right with those you've offended also.

    The second part of my prayer time is **praise;** something I believe we don't do enough. We don't praise the Lord or thank Him enough for all the blessings in our lives. Most of our prayers consist of what I call 'give-me's. Give me this, and give me that. Won't you stop long enough to thank and praise the Lord for His many blessings and how He's answered prayer? I hope you will.

    The third part of my prayer time is **talking,** which is really just sharing different requests for my family, myself, others, pastors and other people. The Lord already knows your heart, but there's something special about releasing our cares to Him as He cares for us. He loves it when we spend time with Him.

    The last part of my prayer time is **listening.** That's the really hard part. If you're asking for wisdom and guidance, you have to stay around long enough to listen to receive God's answer to your prayer. You won't always get an answer right then, but you need to stick around long enough to hear His voice and get direction.

I would like to recommend a book to you called *Partners in Prayer* by John Maxwell. I encourage you to get the book and become a prayer partner for your pastor and staff. Those in ministry have different arrows coming at them than what the average church member sitting in the church pew has. They have a lot more demands on their personal time, their life and their family time. You need to lift them up in prayer and encourage them. That's what this book talks about. John Maxwell's church of 1,000 exploded because of the power of prayer. Prayer became the catalyst that launched their church in reaching the community and those around them for Christ.

- **Read in a Christian book daily.** "Leaders are readers, and readers are leaders." Reading in a Christian book will help to encourage you, challenge you, and motivate you to become all you can be with God's help. Men need to be the leaders in their home when it comes to spiritual matters.

Here's a thought to close on, because this is something many of us struggle with. Time and fatigue can become our excuses for not being the leader we need to be. It's easy to let the pressures of life keep us from our most important priorities...time with God and time with our family. Let's do our best to teach our families about spiritual things and take the special moments God gives us to make true life impact.

"Time and fatigue can become our excuses for not being the leader we need to be.

Chapter 6

Communicate With Your Wife!

One of the best gifts you could ever give your wife is truly listening and truly talking to her! She needs meaningful conversation. She needs you to listen and comprehend what she is saying. Listening and comprehending are two different animals. Comprehending happens when you completely understand what she is saying. It's not just hearing the words or repeating them back like a good little parrot. Listening is the hardest part of communication.

Build your "friendship" with your wife. When you truly communicate, you are doing this. When you were dating, you were friends at first. You had fun; you did things together. That turned into love, and the relationship blossomed. Sharing and listening develops the close friendship aspect of your marriage. Women thrive on building relationships. This does not mean having conversations about the kids or what to have for dinner. It is truly sharing your inner thoughts and feelings. How do you feel? Don't hold things in. By sharing your thoughts and feelings, you are showing her she is important to you and that you value her and her opinion. Tell her how your day went at work. She wants to be a part of your life and you a part of hers.

Most men don't naturally thrive on relationships, so men must continually strive to strengthen this area. A man needs to remember if he and his wife are best friends, his wife won't need ten other best friends. What do best friends do? They talk, they listen, they empathize, they understand each other, they don't judge, they don't put each other down, they're honest, and they value each other and what they have to say. Best friends have a common bond together. A husband and wife should be each other's best friend.

She needs to be able to trust you and feel secure. Is there anything you are afraid to talk about? Openness means spilling your guts out to your spouse. Most men are afraid to reveal their true feelings, because they don't want to appear weak or stupid. However guys, it is just the opposite. Men must make themselves vulnerable and transparent, because this is where true intimacy is birthed.

Studies show that women have a vocabulary of 20,000–25,000 words a day. Men have a vocabulary of about 10,000–12,000 words a day, about half as many. Some women believe they have twice as many words because they have to repeat everything twice to their husbands! Suppose a couple has small children and the wife is at home during the day. When the man gets home from work, he may have already used up his "words" for the day; but guess how many this wife still has left... about 20,000–25,000 words ready to go. That doesn't mean the husband needs to set the timer and say to his wife, "Okay dear, you have thirty minutes to get all your 20,000 words out. Go!" That wouldn't work too well, would it? That's not the sensitivity that is needed. Your wife has a specific need to talk and share when it comes to communication.

> *"Men must make themselves vulnerable and transparent, because this is where true intimacy is birthed."*

Men also need to remember that their wives sometimes just want them to listen and not necessarily to "fix" their problems. This can be difficult because men tend to be conquerors. They want to be given a task and to complete it. Men tend to go from one thing to the next and "fix" or conquer the task. When a wife goes to her husband and tells him about a problem she's having, he tends to "fix" the problem by telling her what she needs to do to take care of it. He's gone into the "fix-it mode". The next day the wife shares the same problem with him. He responds by saying, "I've already told you what you need to do. If you're not going to listen to me, then don't ask for my advice." At this point the wife becomes frustrated, and the husband becomes confused. This is called cross communication.

Men tend to listen with their heads; women tend to speak from their hearts with feelings and emotions. If a wife is speaking from her heart and her husband is listening with his head trying to "fix" the problem, it will make them both frustrated. When a wife is ready to talk to her husband, she needs to help him out by communicating to him whether to help her "fix" it or if she just wants him to listen. He can then know if he needs to listen with his head and put it in the "fix it mode" to repair a problem, or if he needs to listen with his heart and put it in the "heart mode" as his wife shares what is on her heart by sharing her feelings and emotions. Guys, you can also ask your wife if she needs help fixing the problem or if she just wants you to listen while she shares. This will let you know what filter to listen with and how to respond. One couple told me the husband will ask, "What do you need right now?" This helps them pinpoint the area, communicate effectively and proves to be very helpful. Women are emotional creatures. What they think and how they feel is what makes them tick. By listening, you can show your wife you value her, her feelings and what she shares is important to you. You show her you care by sharing your lives with each other by means of conversation like best friends would do.

Chapter 7

Help With the Household Duties and Children!

Sometimes your wife would appreciate you helping out around the house more than she would appreciate flowers or a gift. Your actions in this area speak volumes. Sometimes the most romantic thing you can do is to come home and clean the toilets. You may be wondering, "Joe, what in the world do romance and toilets have in common? It just doesn't jive." The jobs around your house are not just your wife's jobs, they are yours too. My hand fits a toilet brush as well as anybody's. When we've been traveling and return home, I clean the toilets, which is something my wife hates to do. I don't like to dust, so she does that. If your wife is busy working and trying to take care of everything, and you come home and sit in the recliner most of the evening, there's an imbalance. You may not know it, but this is building up resentment in your wife. Picture this...You've been sitting in your recliner most of the night. Your wife has been in the kitchen working away making dinner and then getting things cleaned up. You come up to her and start hugging and rubbing on her. You say, "Baby, you are fine. You sure are a sweet thang." Guess what she's thinking now? Something like, "I know what he wants now," and do you know what else she's thinking? "Not on your life!" She doesn't feel loved and respected, because she's tired and has been trying to take care of everything while you sat and relaxed all evening. If this

> *"Here is the point...you need to work together and then relax together."*

is the case in your house, you need to take a hard look at yourself. You are being selfish. Here is the point...you need to work together and then relax together. If you both work to get things done, then you can spend couple time together.

If both you and your wife work outside the home, then you need to divide up the list of chores and work together to get them done. If you have children, assign them age-appropriate tasks to do as well. This not only helps get the jobs done, but teaches them responsibility. It shows your kids they are not the center of the family, but that they are part of the family team. Plus, it will teach them some of the life skills they will need to know after they're grown and have a home of their own. I suggest you pick a week night to get things done so the weekends are free to spend time together as a family. Otherwise, you will dread weekends and the time spent together because it just means work and no time to have fun. Let them look forward to family time. It should mean a fun time for everyone.

There are two reasons why helping out is so important: First, it shows your wife you value her and appreciate all that she does. Second, it gets the daily responsibilities out of the way sooner so you can spend quality time together as a couple and as a family.

Chapter 8

Stay Attractive To Your Wife

Most women aren't visually aroused, but it sure doesn't hurt for you to look good to your wife. Not only will you look good for your wife, but you'll probably be healthier and feel better about yourself as well. This isn't a bad thing for either of you!

Have you ever heard about the Dunlap Disease? It's where your belly has dun-lapped over your belt. Ha-ha At a conference I had one gentleman tell me he had "Furniture Disease." I asked him what that was, and he said, "My chest has fallen into my drawers." I laughed till I cried. I wonder how many of us could fit into the tuxedo we wore at our wedding. Do you dress sloppy? Do you shave for your wife even when it's not a work day? My wife and boys hate it when I don't shave. I won't get any hugs or kisses that day from any of them because they say my whiskers hurt. Now dads, it's important to pass along the tradition of the whisker rubs we got from our dads, right? When we are tickling and hugging at bedtime, my boys will say, "Oooh, Dad, your whiskers hurt me. You are a wooly booger." I hate shaving just

"Not only will you look good for your wife, but you'll probably be healthier and feel better about yourself as well."

like the next guy, but I know when I do, I will get more hugs and kisses. I know I'm more attractive to Debbie when I shave, so I do it even on vacation.

Staying attractive in all aspects of your personal appearance just may encourage an improved sex life. Some of you may take this to the extreme and start shaving four-to-five times a day. You'll have nicks all over your face, but you'll be smiling! The point is this...You want to look good to your wife. Ask her for her input on how to accomplish that.

Chapter 9

Truly Show Her That You Value Her and That You Value Her Opinions

In my opinion, this point is probably #1 on both the men's and women's side. You can tell it on a wife's face if she feels valued and loved by her husband. Guys, we need to make sure our wives know they are the most important person in our lives apart from our relationship with Jesus Christ! Many women get the impression from their husbands that their work is more of a priority than they are. Most women feel like they are in competition with your work. If your wife calls you at work and it's not a good time to talk, tell her that and then call her back as soon as you can. Remember to call her back because your wife called for a specific reason. When she calls you at work, pay attention and listen. If you would listen the first time, she might not have to call you 10 times for the same thing. She needs to know she's important even when you're busy at work. You are showing her she's more important than your work, or anything else. I feel you should call your wife at least once a day just to see how she's doing and let her know you're thinking of her. It's nice to get a call saying, "I was thinking about you and wanted to let you know I love and miss you."

"You can tell it on a wife's face if she feels valued and loved by her husband."

At first she might say, "Okay...will you please put my husband on the phone. This sounds like him, but I haven't heard those words in a long time".

Treat your wife as a team member and not a player sitting on the sidelines. She's not a babysitter, waitress or maid. Your wife is your M-A-T-E, not your M-A-I-D! She wants to be appreciated, respected and admired by you! Marriage is a relationship—not a project to be completed. When you take care of and nurture her (wanting her to grow and feel secure in your love and in the Lord's love), you are in a way taking care of yourself. You are one in God's eyes. She is a gift from the Lord to you. She needs you to be committed to her and your kids. You should treat her as a priceless gift or a treasure. She is a part of the team, and not a doormat. Your wife can complement you in so many ways and makes you complete.

She wants to be appreciated, respected and admired by you. When is the last time you told her how much you truly appreciated all she does? Look daily for things you can appreciate about your wife or the things she does. I urge you to make a list of all the things she does. Tell her thank you and praise her about something daily. Can anyone be appreciated or valued too much? This is an area that can only help a marriage. Actually, there is a lot of power in praise.

Another way to show your wife you value her is to give her plenty of hugs and kisses...affection. I'm talking about reaching for her hand, putting your arm around her waist and opening her car door. You know, they didn't stop putting a handle on the passenger side of the car. This is a way to get back that animal attraction you once had. Most men give hugs and kisses when they want it to lead to the bedroom. If a husband approaches his wife and makes an advance or a suggestive comment, she knows what's coming next...the bedroom. True affection is hugging, kissing and touching without wanting it to lead to something else. A wife needs hugs and kisses, and genuine affection, without it leading to something else. You need to display this affection without having resentment built up in her. You don't want your wife thinking, "Great...I know what's he's wanting now. I know what's coming next and now I'm really put in a predicament. If I say no, he's going to get aggravated; if I say yes, I'm going

"Do things for your wife to show you love her for who she is...not for what she can give."

to feel used because I don't feel valued, appreciated and loved." That's a tough place for your wife to be. Guys give intimacy to get sex, and women give sex to get intimacy.

When a puppy does a trick, what does he want? A treat, right? Guys, you have to be careful in this area so when it's bedtime you don't say, "I did this and this to show you that I love you. Now, may I have my treat?"

You're standing there with your tongue sticking out panting like a dog waiting for a treat. Do things for your wife to show you love her for who she is...not for what she can give. She can tell the difference.

Proverbs 5:15 states, "Drink water from your own cistern and fresh water (flowing) from your own well." This is talking about our sexual lives. But...before you get water out of the ground, it takes effort and work to get to it. You've got to dig the well before you drink the water. You have to do the work before you get the refreshment. The same is true in a couple's sexual life. You have to prime the pump. You have to treat your spouse well. You have to make your spouse feel valued before this area can flow. The efforts you put into your sexual relationship are well worth the benefits you will reap from them.

Men, where does sex start in your home? It starts with you each morning. This means treating her as the priceless jewel she is. This symbolizes security, protection, comfort, and approval. Something so little — means so much. The main reason a couple has sexual problems is that they have an absence of romantic love. For women, sex is a mind thing. How have you treated your wife in the last 24 hours. Does she feel loved and valued by you?

Try this sometime. Go to your wife and kiss her like you haven't for a long time. Now, I'm talking about a REAL kiss, not just a peck. (Brush your teeth before you do this...it will bless her.) Tell her you love her and you're so glad she's your wife...and then, walk away. She'll stand there dazed and stagger for a minute because she's not used to something like that and she'll wonder why you didn't want anything more. As you walk away, she will think to herself, "What a wonderful guy I'm married to!" Your wife needs non-sexual touches just because you love her for who she is. She needs to know you value her!

Chapter 10

Put Your Wife's Needs First

You are your wife's servant. This includes even the little things. Do you consistently have to have the last piece of pizza, the last cookie, the last candy bar? Are you looking out for yourself instead of saying, "Here, honey, you take it. I want you to have it." You need to display an attitude that puts your spouse's needs first even in the small insignificant things. This doesn't mean you need to have a martyr mentality, but an attitude to serve. It's a heart thing. The attitude of your heart is shown by your actions and by your words.

How about the husband who says this to his wife, "Honey, you know I love you with all of my heart, you're so beautiful, and I would rather

> **"The attitude of your heart is shown by your actions and by your words."**

be with you and our family more than anything, but I'm going to play sports, hang out with my buddies, go golfing/hunting/fishing/riding, etc. again this weekend. Ya'll have a great weekend." A lot of women feel like they are golf widows, sports widows, hunting widows, fishing widows, motorcycle widows, etc. Something that is consistently taking you away from your family is not a good thing. It's fine to have hobbies...in moderation. However; if your hobbies are consistently taking away from your quality family time, then your actions are saying you love a particular hobby or activity more than you love your wife and family. Many women feel like they're second class to their husband's recreational activities, and then resentment will build up between the two of them. You may be saying all of those nice things to your wife and family, but your true desires come out in your actions. It all boils down to the attitude of the heart. What is your heart's attitude? You need to put your wife's and family's needs first. This is exactly what your wife sees in your actions. Your actions speak louder than your words! Hobbies are a good stress reliever, but make sure your family is your first priority!

Remember in Ephesians 5, the Bible says a husband is to love his wife like Christ loved the church and gave Himself for her. The first thing most men think about in this verse is that they would give their lives for their families as Christ gave up his life. A man has the natural instinct to protect, and this is especially true for his family. You would put yourself in harms way, pull a family member from the path of an oncoming car, or put yourself in front of the car to protect your family. I'd like us to look at this passage a little deeper. When Jesus died on the cross, whose needs did he put first? He put our needs first. As the old hymn says, "He could have called ten thousand angels to destroy the world and set him free." Jesus Christ willingly died for you and for me. His heart was, "Father, not my will, but yours be done." His heart was right and willing to serve to the death. He came to serve...not to be served. Jesus was first and foremost a servant. His heart was for others...not for himself. As men, that's what our heart should be in our families. We need to put our family's needs first. As husbands, we are to put the needs of our wives first and be unselfish for them.

Chapter 11

Be Thoughtful and Romantic

Thoughtful doesn't necessarily mean expensive. When you are putting the needs of your wife first, you will automatically look for ways to be thoughtful. When was the last time you surprised your wife with flowers, a card, or something special? This doesn't have to be expensive, just thoughtful. This could be writing a note and putting it on her pillow. It could be doing something you know she doesn't enjoy doing, such as a chore or errand. It is anything that shows thoughtfulness. Be creative. Do you remember the example of the store-bought arrangement of flowers vs. the picked flowers? Which will be appreciated more by your wife? The picked flowers, because they took thought and time. They were also free!

When Debbie and I were newlyweds and married just a few years, we lived in Jacksonville, Florida. We didn't have any children at the time. There was a five month period when I didn't have income coming in. Here's why...I deliberately left the job I had to look for God's will in my employment. I was making a transition from a job to a career. It's hard for a man to be without a job. When two men meet for the first time, the first question they normally ask is, "What do you do for a living?" In many ways, a man's job is his sense of self-esteem. When a man doesn't have a job, not only does his self-esteem go down to zero, sometimes he dips below that level. That man will begin to ask himself if he's worth anything. He wonders if anyone will give him a chance. He begins to think of himself as not being worthwhile, but as being worthless. If you're in that position, you need to stay with it; be persistent. God's Word says to ask, seek and knock...not to sit, wait and hope. When I found myself in this position, I was out knocking on doors and was diligent at it. The whole time Debbie was behind me, telling me she loved and supported me. She was my encourager. If your spouse is going through this, now is the time they need you more than ever. Your spouse needs you to encourage them to stay out there looking for the position God has for them.

Debbie was working full time, and we had some money in savings, but we didn't want to touch it. We wanted to live within our means. In other words, we didn't want to spend more than we had coming in. This is a simple financial principle that would keep a lot of couples out of financial debt. We didn't want to live off credit cards or to deplete our savings account. Debbie was paid once a month, and it was a long time between paychecks, especially when you're looking for that paycheck to come in.

I remember one month in particular after Debbie got paid. We had paid all the bills, and we each had $1.00 left to last for the whole month. I was so thankful to Debbie for what she was doing, I took my dollar and bought her a card. In the card I thanked her for encouraging me and for supporting us during that time. I dropped off the card to her when I was in the area of her work handing out resumes. Do you think she still has that card? You better believe it! Did that card cost a lot? That is a trick question. It didn't cost a lot because it was only $1.00, but it really did, because that was everything I had for an entire month and she knew it. The point is this...it's not how much you spend, but it's the thought that goes behind it. Some of Debbie's favorite gifts are the ones that cost the least, but the thought behind it means everything to her.

"The point is this...it's not how much you spend, but it's the thought that goes behind it."

Some guys say that they aren't good with remembering dates for birthdays or anniversaries. We remember what we want to remember! Get a day-timer or something to help. You must remember your wife on special occasions. At our house for birthdays, we draw birthday signs and tape them up all over the house. A big hint to guys—don't buy your wife anything with an electrical cord attached to it for her birthday, anniversary or Christmas!

Chapter 12

Keep Your "Honey-Do" List Current

Your wife needs to be proud of her home. Your wife's home is her nest, so to speak. Keep your home in good repair, so your wife can be proud of it. It makes her feel overwhelmed and depressed when things aren't in good order. More than likely she will become frustrated with you when the list gets very long. Prioritize the items and tackle them one at a time. Guys, do you wonder why your wife sometimes nags you? If you would work to keep your honey-do-list cur-

> *"Prioritize the items and tackle them one at a time."*

rent, your wife wouldn't continually have to "nag" you to get things done. Guys, do your part. This is the main reason your wife resorts to nagging. She feels it is the only way to get you to get things done. If you would act like a man, your wife wouldn't have to treat you like a little boy. A husband shouldn't turn his wife into a nag; he just needs to tackle what's on the list so she doesn't have to remind him. Now, guys, I put more things on my honey-do-list than my wife does. Many women get the bad reputation of loading up the list, but it's usually things we are too lazy to do and want to overlook. Try this. Say you have five things that really need to get done. Take a list of the five things to your wife and ask her to prioritize them in order of importance to her. This gives you a prioritized list and by asking her input even when it's just prioritizing the list, you are showing you value her and you value her input.

You might be asking, "Joe, is this really that important?" At a conference, I had a lady who shared with me during the workshop time for couples; she ranked this as #1 of her needs. She then went further, and put percentages by each category to fine tune it. She ranked this area #1 to her and it carried 70% of the total weight of her needs. If you were her husband and you wanted to be irresistible to her, can you figure out what

might work? This is the kind of blueprint or map you can get as you rank
these categories and discuss them with your spouse.

Chapter 13

Provide Financially For Your Family

Are you watching your finances? Are you providing for the needs of your family? Do you have more month than paycheck? If you are consistently counting on credit cards to make it from month to month, you are committing financial suicide. Paying the minimums is not going to pay off the credit cards. You can't keep living off credit cards. If you are, you've got to make some changes. Remember, if you keep doing what you're doing, you will keep getting what you're getting. To get different results, something has to change. I'm not trying to throw stones at anyone if you're carrying debt or trying to put guilt on you, but credit card debt will eat your lunch! Whether you realize it or not, financial stress will put a strain on your marriage. We always hear that finances are one of the top things that tear marriages apart. That is true, so this area needs major attention. I'm not saying you should cut up all of your credit cards. (Although, some need to do that.) Our rule of thumb for a credit card is this...We don't charge anything unless we have the cash to pay for it. Charging it means I don't have the cash with me. If we can't pay the bill in full when it comes in, then we don't use the charge card.

When you're purchasing things and living beyond your means, you're putting a strain on your marriage. What it boils down to is whether you want 'things' or a strong relationship. When you get ready to make a purchase, you need to ask yourself, "Is this a need or a want?" Picture a set of scales in front of you like the

"...you need to ask yourself, "Is this a need or a want?"

scales of justice. It has the arm across the top with chains hanging down and cups at the end of each side of the chains. On one side is needs, and on the other side is wants. Before you make a purchase you need to ask yourself this question, "Is this a need or a want?" There are definite needs a family has like toothpaste, deodorant, food, automobile, etc. We may need a new car, but we may not need a Mercedes. A cheaper car is still an automobile; however, it's not a need to have the Mercedes. If you have the funds for a Mercedes, that's fine. If you don't, you need to ask yourself if the purchase is a need or a want. If you have a lot of wants and the purchase of those wants is going to put stress on your marriage, then the ultimate answer needs to be "No." I pray you won't choose 'things' over a stronger marriage and family.

Many times a husband will comment on how much money his wife is spending. If you look at what women spend the money on, you will see that she's usually not buying things for herself. Rather, she is buying things for the family, such as food, clothes and other things the family needs. Husbands need to be careful not to accuse their wives of spending all the money. You need to remember that it's because of what she does there is food in the house, shoes on the kids' feet and so on.

When it comes to finances, give yourself a 24-hour cool down period before making a major investment or purchase. We are part of an instant society and tend to buy things impulsively. You need to step back and allow yourself 24 hours to consider what you're doing. Pray about it. Ask the Lord, "What would You have me to do? What would You have me to purchase with **your** money?"

When we lived in Georgia, we started the newlywed ministry at our church. One week in Sunday School we had a lesson on finances and God's perspective of our money. The next week one of the young couples shared what God had done in their heart during the week. They had gone to some friend's house the weekend before the lesson on finances. Their young friends had brand new furniture that looked great, smelled good—the whole bit. Things were tight financially for this couple, but they knew they had a few 'extra' dollars each month. They caught the furniture fever. They went out and bought a whole new room of furniture. Within a day of them ordering the furniture, we had the lesson on finances, the importance of the 24-hour cool down period, and not being strapped for each last dollar. The Holy Spirit spoke to their hearts, and they called on the Monday, following the lesson, to cancel their furniture order. You could have heard a pin drop as they shared that story with the class the following week. What a powerful lesson for everyone there! That couple is now in full-time ministry, and we are so proud of them. They 'taught' the whole class the importance of waiting on God.

God doesn't own just the 10% tithe He requires, He also owns the other 90%. If it's all His and we're getting ready to make a major investment with His money and resources He's entrusted to us, don't you think we need to step back at least 24-hours and ask Him what He would have us to do? That pretty much changes the perspective doesn't it? Many times when you step back and ask for His guidance, He will put something better, nicer, or less expensive in your path. We tend to be in such a hurry that we end up getting God's "good," but we miss out on God's "best." Are you in such a hurry to do things or buy things on your terms and timing that you're not stepping back and asking God what He wants you to do? Try waiting at least 24 hours, seek God and get His best for your family and your life!

There are some great resources out there to help you in this area. Check these out:

www.daveramsey.com
www.crown.org

Application Time

As we go into the application time, here's an example I think will help you as we talk about specific needs for both men and women. Picture a nice shiny gold chain. It looks good, and it's in good condition. None of the links are weak, and it's not broken. Where is a chain normally going to break? It will break at its weakest link. The importance of a chain is that every link depends on the next one to give it strength. The links are dependent on each other. The needs for both men and women are like those links. Each link is dependent on the next to hold the chain together and give it strength.

Let me ask you a question. If you had a chain, like the one above, which represented your marriage, what would your "chain of marriage" look like?

1. Would it be shiny and strong with the links in good condition? This chain gets shined every day. This means you never stop working on your marriage. You keep the line of communication open. You're willing to look for changes you can make to better yourself and your marriage. You go to marriage events and read books on improving your marriage.

2. Would it look good, but tarnished a little? This marriage might just have lost the sparkle it once had. All it needs is some cleaning up. Too many times we sweep problems under a rug thinking it will go away. The best way to fix it is to clean it up before it gets to be a bigger mess. Attack the problem, not the person and fix it now.

3. Is it a fake 14k gold necklace? Does it look shiny on the outside, but deep down there are some links very close to breaking? This marriage looks good on the surface, but behind closed doors it is falling apart. You put on a good fake smile to impress the people around you, but you're really hurting on the inside.

4. Would the chain be in one piece, but all scratched up? This is one that needs to be dipped in gold again before it can shine. There are so many scars and no forgiveness. The past keeps coming up and won't die. You have to stop harboring thoughts and quit bringing the topic up. You can't forget the wrongs done to you, but you can

forgive. This one needs a big dose of forgiveness, so let God dip it in His grace.

5. Would it already be broken at a link and need immediate repair? A chain can't work the way it was intended to work when it is broken. You need to take it to the Heavenly jeweler for Him to fix. You need help — maybe a Christian counselor. Don't let pride get in the way of you getting help when needed.

6. Some of you might say, "Joe, if you were to take the chain and rip it apart as hard as you could with links flying everywhere — that would be my marriage!" I can tell you this under the authority of God's Word...(regardless of the state of your marriage)... it is not God's plan for you to get a new chain. It is His plan for you to repair the one you have — the one He gave you.

Remodeling work is hard. If you've done it before, you probably just said, "Amen!" I believe remodeling is so hard because you have to take out the old before you can put in the new. Taking out the old is real tough sometimes, because you're dealing with a lot of imperfections. Let's apply this to our marriages. We all have areas we need to improve, but we must learn to take out the old first. Don't leave your marriage empty by just taking out the old, but replace the space with new and fresh ways to make your relationship work. I really believe the following ways to be irresistible will help you in making your marriage the best it can be for God's glory!

Application Time — The Irresistible Husband

Ladies...rank these categories in order of importance to you from 1 to 9. Number 1 will be what is most important to you. Discuss each topic with your husband and explain why this is a priority to you and why it makes you feel loved:

_____ **Be a spiritual leader.**

What is your spouse currently doing in this area that you like?
....
....
....

What are some suggestions you can give your spouse to improve in this area?
....
....
....

_____ **Communicate with your wife.**

What is your spouse currently doing in this area that you like?
....
....
....

What are some suggestions you can give your spouse to improve in this area?
....
....
....

_____ **Help with the household duties and children when needed.**

What is your spouse currently doing in this area that you like?
....
....
....

What are some suggestions you can give your spouse to improve in this area?
....
....
....

_____ **Stay attractive to your wife.**

What is your spouse currently doing in this area that you like?

....
....
....

What are some suggestions you can give your spouse to improve in this area?

....
....
....

_____ **Truly show her that you value HER and that you value her opinions.**

What is your spouse currently doing in this area that you like?

....
....
....

What are some suggestions you can give your spouse to improve in this area?

....
....
....

_____ **Put your wife's needs first.**

What is your spouse currently doing in this area that you like?

....
....
....

What are some suggestions you can give your spouse to improve in this area?

....
....
....

_____ **Be thoughtful and romantic.**

What is your spouse currently doing in this area that you like?

....
....
....

What are some suggestions you can give your spouse to improve in this area?

....

....

....

_____ **Keep your honey-do-list current.**

What is your spouse currently doing in this area that you like?

....

....

....

What are some suggestions you can give your spouse to improve in this area?

....

....

....

_____ **Provide financially for your family.**

What is your spouse currently doing in this area that you like?

....

....

....

What are some suggestions you can give your spouse to improve in this area?

....

....

....

PART THREE

THE IRRESISTIBLE WIFE

HOW TO MEET THE SEVEN BASIC NEEDS OF YOUR HUSBAND

A wife can make herself irresistible to her husband by learning to meet some specific needs. Ladies, your husbands will get a chance at the end of this session to rank these areas in order of importance to him, like you did, so remember to listen intently to what he'll be sharing with you. This will be a blueprint to know what makes your husband feel most loved and respected. Remember, I'm not covering these in any particular order...are you ready...here we go!

Chapter 14

He Needs Regular Sex

I know what you're thinking, "Great...here we go with the sex stuff. That's all guys think about." I may surprise you by saying it's NOT all they think about, but I believe most women don't realize how crucial this area is in your marriage. This is something he can't do without!

The question I usually get asked at this point is, "Joe, could you define regular?" This is usually one of those "laughing till you cry" moments at our live events, but let me do my best to answer this question. First of all, I'm not going to recommend any weekly or monthly quotas, because I know exactly what the guys would do. It would come to Saturday night and the husband would say something like this to his wife, "You know honey, Joe told us the average was _____ times a week. Well, it's the end of the week, and you know we have some catching up to do!"

Debbie and I were watching an interview of a lady on TV whose husband had been unfaithful. The interviewer asked her if she had any clue this was going on. She responded she had no clue whatsoever that he was having an affair. The interviewer then proceeded to ask her how long it had been since she and her husband had been intimate. She responded with, "About a year." Hello! This was a major red flag. So, if it's been a year for you...it's time! I'm not trying to be crude with this area, because it's a beautiful area God has designed for marriage. Women need to understand the real significance here.

A common complaint women have is that their husbands want them to be more aggressive and initiate sex. The best way I know how to answer this is with a classic story I heard Dr. Danny Aiken tell at a marriage conference. He had a lady come up after a conference and ask him, "How can I get past this issue once and for all with my husband wanting me to be more aggressive and initiate sex." He told her to go home and pursue her husband like an animal for the next three weeks. He asked her to call him after the three weeks were up. She said, "You've got to be kidding me. You mean if I do that it will change this area in our marriage?" He told her it would, so she decided to try it. In essence, she seduced her husband at any time she could. When the kids were in bed, she would put on something her husband would like. She did this for three weeks like he suggested, and then called him back. She said, "I did what you told me. As we speak right now, my husband is in the corner of our bedroom, crouched down, waiving a white hanky, saying, "I can't take any more…I give in." Ladies, you might want to try this three-week experiment. I'm sure your husband wouldn't mind.

A lot of times in the sexual area, couples are like windshield wipers on a car. They may be moving, but they don't get any closer to each other.

> *"Sometimes we can be going through the motions, but never really building intimacy and oneness in this area."*

Sometimes we can be going through the motions, but never really building intimacy and oneness in this area. Instead of chasing each other, couples need to come together and talk about it.

Women are like crock pots and men are like microwaves. Like crock pots, they stay warm a while later too. Remember, for most women sex starts out as an emotional thing and then becomes a physical thing. It is just the opposite for men. For most men, sex starts out as a physical thing and then it's emotional. God didn't make us the same; he made us different on purpose.

The physical relationship and how God made us is absolutely beautiful. God has said the marriage bed is undefiled. It's something we don't need to be ashamed of in our marriages. It's something to be kept private and not shared with others; but there is no reason to be ashamed. It's beautiful because it's something God created for marriage.

Women, when was the last time you initiated sex? When was the last time you talked about and listened to your husband in this area? Ladies want their husbands to read their minds during sex. That is not possible. You have to learn to talk and help each other discover a satisfying and enjoyable physical relationship.

Is your husband an animal? Some of you may think he is, but he's trying to let you know he desperately needs this area to be strong in your marriage. If your husband picks and pinches at you, it's because he needs something. You should be glad he picks and pinches you, because it means he is attracted to you! He wants you to be as interested in sex as he is and even sometimes be the instigator.

Ladies, I want you to really pay attention to this next analogy. I want you to block everything else out so you can comprehend it. Picture this scenario: you enter a restaurant and you're waiting to be seated. While you're waiting, you happen to see the dessert tray and it looks so delicious. Have you ever picked out your dessert before the meal? We love sweets in our home, so it's easy for me to imagine this. You happen to see a certain dessert that really gets your attention. Now, I'm partial to the hot fudge brownie with ice cream. They get a bowl right out of the warmer and put a big piece of brownie in it that has just come out of the oven. So now you have the warm brownie in the warm bowl and then they put vanilla bean ice cream on top. The ice cream hits the warm brownie and the warm bowl and it starts to melt a little and gets soft around the edges so you have a little bit of soft ice cream in every bite. It's not done yet. Next comes the hot fudge and whipped cream on top. You see that dessert before your meal and you say, "That's what I'm having when my meal is done." Well, you get seated and eat your delicious meal. It tastes so good you have a bit of trouble stopping before you are very full. Now, they come around with that same dessert tray you drooled over several minutes before. Your response is a little different now, isn't it? Your response is something like, "I can't eat another bite or I'll explode right here and right now! I'm so satisfied—I don't have room for anything else. What once looked so good to me, now looks repulsive." Have you ever been there before? Here's the point...ladies, you are your husband's main course when it comes to sex. If he's so full of you, he won't have room for anything or anyone else. It is easier for him to control his eyes. It's easier for him to resist when the temptation of another comes along who may look tempting. It will look repulsive to him if he's so full of your sweet love!

Proverbs 5:15-21 is talking about our sexual lives. It states, "Drink water from your own cistern and fresh water *(flowing)* from your own well. Should your springs be dispersed abroad, streams of water in the street? Let them be yours alone and not for strangers with you. Let your fountain be blessed, and rejoice in the wife of your youth. As a loving hind and a graceful doe, let her breasts satisfy you at all times; Be exhilarated always with her love. For why should you, my son, be exhilarated with an adulteress *(strange woman)* and embrace the bosom of a foreigner? For the ways of a man are before the eyes of the LORD, and He watches all his paths." (NASV) It tells us to drink water from our own cistern. We're supposed to drink out of our own well, or in other words our own spouse who God has given us. The water that flows into the streets is not to be shared by others; they're to be private between a husband and wife. This means we are not to talk about it with friends, family or anyone else.

Proverbs 27:7 talks about our sexual lives also, being full of honey. "He who is full loathes honey, but to the hungry even what is bitter, tastes sweet." (NIV) When applying this verse, think about the dessert tray scenario. "He who is full loathes honey, ..." Just like the sweet dessert, if a man is full he will hate honey or any other temptation. "...but to the hungry even what is bitter," (such as an adulterous relationship) "...tastes sweet." Because that person is starving, he's willing to settle for less. If your spouse is full of your sweetness, they won't look for anything bitter.

Chapter 15

He Needs You To Listen and Comprehend What He Is Saying

Are you so preoccupied with taking care of the children and other things that you're not giving your husband the time he really deserves? You need to be his best friend. You need to be willing to truly listen to your husband and not be so busy with everything else that is going on.

I know some wives who say their husbands won't ever talk to them. How can they when they are on the phone all night talking to family members, friends, neighbors, etc. When you are constantly on the phone, this shows your husband that building relationships with others is more important to you than building your relationship with him. When he is at home, that's your time to build your relationship. Don't accuse him of not talking if you don't give him the time. **We really try to guard our time at night in our home since that is our main time we have to be together as a family.**

Men are recreational creatures; they like to play and have fun. Wives need to get into their husbands' world from time to time and hang out doing what he likes to do. Let's say there's some special game he wants to watch on TV. Offer to make some of his favorite foods and get his favorite drink for him to enjoy while watching the event. Let him know you want to sit with him and watch it together. He'll look at you funny—like, "You look like my wife, but I've never heard you say those words before." Just be sure to wait until the event is over before asking him any questions. That will be a blessing to him. Go fishing with him or whatever he enjoys doing. Spend time with him letting him know you are his best friend by getting into his world.

You must come up with a good time when you can both talk and share. Remember to "clock out" like in the couple time model we already discussed. It's hard to talk when the kids are young, running around, or when it's time for supper. Maybe you should wait until they are in bed. Make a list throughout the day about things you want to discuss, so you don't forget anything. Work at trying to provide couple time for each other. By making 'couple time,' you get around the two biggest hindrances to communication which are 1) Lack of time and 2) Being tired. By making time earlier in the evening, you aren't tired when you're talking. Most couples talk late at night at 10:00 to 11:00 and it turns into "intense moments of fellowship." You're tired and ready for bed. Remember, if you have older children, share with them the concept of "couple time." Let them know for a specific amount of time each evening, the two of you are going to be talking to each other and you do not want to be interrupted. Make it clear to them that this is your time. Your kids will test you on this. You need to make this time flexible but you need to plan to make it happen. If you don't plan it, it won't happen! This will help you to maximize your time together as a couple and to give each other quality time instead of leftover time. I hope you'll truly try the "couple time" model...We've heard from many husbands and wives how this has worked for them.

Ladies tend to be overcommitted and it pulls them away from their family. Don't let life's busy schedule tear you and your husband apart. How can you listen and comprehend what your husband is saying when you are too busy rushing around trying to be super woman? When things get overwhelming, stop and have a priority check. Take some responsibilities away. Being room mom, participating in Bible studies, volunteering for this and that, having your kids involved in a lot of extra activities, being involved in activities in the community or at church, etc. are all good things, but they could be tools the devil uses to tear your family apart. **In my opinion, busyness is the number one tool the devil uses to tear families apart.** Remember to keep the main thing (your relationship to God, husband, and kids) the main thing. So many of us find ourselves off track. Some wait until scars are so deep, it is hard to fix. Please don't let yourself be overcommitted. Proverbs 11:1 says, "A false balance is an abomination to the LORD. But a just weight is His delight." (NASV) Keep a good balance of the duties

"...busyness is the number one tool the devil uses to tear families apart."

which take your time away from the 'main thing." Maybe you need to work smarter at home, stay at home, leave the TV off, stay off the phone (let the answering machine work for you), or stay focused. You might need to stop all extra activities all together, and work on just your family. Don't keep going till it is too late. There is

"There is no activity that is worth losing your family for."

no activity that is worth losing your family for. What's more important to you, your activities or your family?

Chapter 16

Promote Him In His Career

Are you cheering your husband on? This is his sense of self-worth. A man's job is a large part of his self-esteem. You need to help promote him in his career—don't pull him back. You need to be his cheerleader. Now, you don't have to literally put on a cheerleading outfit and meet him at the door cheering with pom-poms in your hands. (You can try that some time though...he might like it.) You need to realize the importance of your positive words. Be proud of him for what he does. Encourage him to be all he can be for the Lord at his job. To most women, a job is income; but to a man, it is their identity. You can help him succeed at work or pull him down. You play such a BIG part in this area!

Ladies, watch your words—never let them be negative. With your words, you can tear down or build up. He desperately needs you to use your words positively in this area. Be proud of him. Tell him you are proud of him and for what he does to provide for you and your family. Thank him for doing his job and providing for you. Encourage him to succeed.

You need to learn to be content with what you have right now. If you're constantly saying that you need more things—"We need new this and new that." Little do you know, but this puts pressure on your husband. This makes him feel like he is failing to provide for your needs. Are you consumed with possessions and do you put pressure on your husband financially? He just wants to please you more than you know! He wants to make you happy. When you mention those things, he's formulating a plan on how to make it happen. It puts pressure on him to work more hours, to make more money or to get that promotion to provide these things. Things don't make you happy; they make you comfortable. By working more, you'll be seeing less of him. You may have more things, but you'll have less of him.

Studies have shown that a man makes 40% more income if his wife kisses him in the morning. Think about this for a minute. Why is that? It shows him your approval and appreciation. When things aren't right at home, it's **not** a good day at work. I had one lady at a conference ask me, "Joe, how much can my husband make if he gets a lot more than a kiss in the morning?" I laughed so hard and told her she would have to do that research herself, but she would have one happy husband!

If you listen to, encourage, and promote your husband in his career, he will more than likely be more satisfied with his job...and he might even get promotions and raises, which isn't a bad side effect either. Of course, this shouldn't be your main objective for your encouragement to him. You need to appreciate your husband for who he already is, not for who he could become if he lived up to your standards.

On another note...watch how much you call your husband at work. Don't call him ten times a day. How can he get anything done? I've heard of ladies who call their husbands even 20-30 times a day and then they're aggravated when their husband works late. Hello?! The poor guy couldn't get anything done during the day with all of the calls. If you want to talk to him a lot, then keep on calling him and you'll have a lot of time to talk when he gets fired from his job. Limit your calls to only a couple of times during the day, and be sensitive to particular busy days or a busy time of the day. Say things like, "I love you, and I'm looking forward to you coming home." That might help motivate him to put it into high gear, so he won't have to work late.

"You need to appreciate your husband for who he already is, not for who he could become if he lived up to your standards."

Chapter 17

Remember, He Married You To Be His Lover, Not His Mother

Many women get into the "nag" routine. When a wife is a **N-A-G,** she is **Not Attractive** to her **Guy.** Yes, he needs to do his part of taking care of the house and helping with the children, but don't stay on his back continually. By constantly complaining or being negative about the same things, you then become a nag. Women can be so critical and judgmental. You need to watch your words to your husband — make sure they are loving words.

> *"Here's the bottom line...when you nag your husband, it reminds him of how he's failing you."*

Here's the bottom line...when you nag your husband, it reminds him of how he's failing you. Not one man likes to fail and he especially doesn't like to hear about it over and over. So many women criticize their husbands, and it's especially damaging when it's done in public. This breaks down your emotional attachment.

Let me give you a funny example to drive this point home. Let's say the trash needs to be taken out. Here's how the reaction changes the longer you are married:

- A couple married one month — "Thank you for taking out the trash, Sugar Baby. I love to see your muscles ripple when you pick up the garbage can. You take such good care of me." Notice, she didn't even have to ask — he took the trash out on his own. Also, notice all the positive and encouraging words.

- A couple married six months — "Hey Sweetie, do you think you could take out the trash when you get some time? I appreciate your help around the house." She had to ask, but the positive and encouraging words are still there.

- A couple married one year—"Hey Honey, would you take out the garbage? It's so full that I can't pick it up. I didn't know this much trash could fit in here." The nagging and negative words start creeping in.
- A couple married three years—"Would you take out the garbage? I already asked you yesterday. It is so full of dirty diapers that it reeks." She's asked twice and the nagging is in full throttle.
- A couple married five years—"Would you stop watching that baseball game and take out the trash? You know there are things around the house that need to be done."
- A couple married seven years—"When are you going to get your lazy self out of that recliner? The trash needs to be taken out, and you have as much garbage around your recliner as there is in the trash can. How many times do I have to ask before you will finally take it out?" This wife is in the advanced stage of nagging. It obviously doesn't work, so why does she keep nagging?

Proverbs has five specific verses that pertain to this topic:
I. Proverbs 9:13 says, "A foolish woman is clamorous (a noisy shouting, a loud continuous noise); She is simple, and knows nothing." (NKJV) Continuous, loud and shouting makes for a foolish woman.
II. Proverbs 19:13 says, "A foolish son is destruction to his father, And the contentions (ideas or points for which a person argues) of a wife are a constant (unchanging, continually recurring) dripping." (NASV) The Holman Standard says it this way; "...and a wife's nagging is an endless dripping." Have you ever tried to concentrate or go to sleep when there is a constant drip running down the down spout of the gutter? How annoying! This is how the Lord describes a nagging woman.
III. Proverbs 21:9 says, "It is better to dwell in a corner of the housetop, than with a brawling (noisy quarreling) woman in a wide house." (KJV) Do you get what this is saying? It is better to live in a small uncomfortable house than in a huge mansion with a nagging wife. That is powerful!

IV. Proverbs 21:19 says, "It is better to dwell in the wilderness, than with a contentious and angry woman." (KJV) The Holman Standard says, "...than with a nagging and hot-tempered wife." This verse is saying it is better to live in the wilderness than to live with an angry, hot-tempered wife. I have talked with many men who can agree with this verse. You can't get mad at anyone for saying this, but God. He's the one who said these true words.

V. Proverbs 25:24 says, "It is better to dwell in a corner of the housetop, than with a brawling (noisy quarreling) woman in a wide house." (KJV) Notice something very important...Proverbs 21:9 and 25:24 say the exact same thing. The Lord is putting an emphasis on this point if He put it in His Word twice. Do you think maybe the Lord is trying to get this particular point across to us?

Let's say the gutters need to be cleaned on your house. There are two different ways to say the same thing. The first way is this; "When are you ever going to get out there and clean out those gutters. They're about to fall off the house. They already have trees growing out of them!" Do you think this will motivate your husband? Probably not. If it does, it will be for the wrong reasons. The second way you could approach this situation is by saying; "Honey, I know you've been real busy. The gutters really need to be cleaned, so I'm available to go out and help you." You don't have to be joined at the hip in everything you do, but if he's busy, you can certainly offer to help him. That will motivate him to get the job done, and it will show you value him.

Would you like to know how to get your husband to change? Here's how...praise his improvements. Be proud of your husband. Admire the man you chose to share your life with. Let me use our previously funny example about the wife nagging her husband to take out the trash to demonstrate how to do this. Let's say he finally takes the trash out. The nagging wife's response would be, "It's about doggone time you took out the trash. I was going to let it fill up the kitchen; and as a matter of fact, I would let it fill up the whole house until you finally decided to take out the trash. Finally you listened to me." That's not much motivation is it? Let's try a more positive and praising response, "Thank you so much for taking out the trash. (While you're clapping your hands for him) I really appreciate your help around the house." Now the clapping is extreme, but I'm trying to get the point across. The bottom line is this...You don't nag your husband into changing, you praise him into changing! It's just the opposite of what most women think and do. If you were to praise your husband, he'd probably think of other things he could do to make you happy. So often, we focus on the negative. I've heard it takes ten positives to offset one negative. Focus on the positive things your husband does, and praise him for each one.

If you find yourself frustrated in this area, I encourage you to examine yourself and to empty you of yourself. Take a hard look at yourself through your husband's eyes. Step out of your life's bubble. Take a look at what you are doing to hinder him or to make him do or not do what you are constantly nagging him about. Look at ways you may be contributing to this frustration. Would your nagging motivate you? Watch how you say things. Is he busy doing jobs you could or should be doing that he can't find the time to do your list? Make sure he isn't expected to do your responsibilities too. When he comes home, he shouldn't have to consistently bathe the kids, fold laundry and cook dinner. If you are a stay at home mom, these are things you should strive to get done. If his plate is very full, find ways to help him. Make sure you are part of the solution and not part of the problem.

Chapter 18

He Needs Your Admiration and Appreciation; In Other Words...Your RESPECT

I believe this is one of the most important areas for a man, so please pay close attention to this point. Let me ask you this. What's holding your husband back from doing more in his work or for the Lord's work? I believe it is one word that holds him back...fear. There is not one man alive today who wants to fail at anything. Taking a step out into the unknown, not knowing what's going to happen and putting his total trust in the Lord is a fearful thing. If a man has a wife who is behind him, truly believes in him, and encourages him, there is no limit to what this man could do! Don't be a negative person who constantly holds him back from being all God wants him to be. No one enjoys being with a negative person. Your admiration and appreciation will help him tremendously, and it is a great motivator for him. It inspires him to achieve more. No one has ever been admired or appreciated too much by their spouse. You can continually give more to your spouse in this area. Find something you can thank or praise him for daily. Try it, and see what happens. By you showing him respect, you are showing him you love him.

> *"If a man has a wife who is behind him, truly believes in him, and encourages him, there is no limit to what this man could do!"*

When I know that Debbie is proud of me, I feel like Superman. Bring on the speeding bullet or train; I can leap tall buildings with ease. When Debbie is proud of me, it gives me confidence and reassurance to take new and bold steps for the Lord. A bond is built when a wife believes in her husband and speaks respectfully about him. This is magnified when you brag on him in public.

Ladies, if you only knew how much power you have in this area, it would stagger you. You have SO much power and influence with your husband when it comes to honest admiration, appreciation and respect. He desperately needs it from you. Let me give you a personal example. When Debbie and I were newlyweds and married just two years, we lived in Jacksonville, FL. We attended a great church and were actively involved in many things. Personally, I had a hard time opening up and talking to Debbie, and also other people, when we were first married. I am shy by nature. A lifetime friend and also my Sunday School teacher, Ronnie Williams, came to me one day and asked me to do some announcements in Sunday school class. I said, "Ronnie, you're my friend. You know I'd do almost anything for you, but I can't get up in front of people. I don't know how to talk. I'm too scared to do that." Guess what Ronnie got me to do? You guessed it, announcements. Then Ronnie came back to me later and said, "Joe, I'm going to be out for a couple weeks on vacation and I'd like for you to teach for me while I'm gone." I quickly responded, "Ronnie, you're my friend. You know I'd do almost anything for you, but I can't get up there and teach. I'm doing announcements already. I don't know how to talk in front of people and share my heart for a whole hour. Announcements are one thing, but teaching is a whole other thing. I'm too scared." Guess what Ronnie got me to do? You guessed it again, teach for him. This led to full-time teaching in Sunday school, which led to corporate training, which led to speaking around the country at marriage and family events.

I want to give you two specific reasons why the Lord allowed me to grow personally and go from making announcements, to teaching, to public speaking. The first reason is this... I can't do this without God's help! I pray that I'm totally emptied of myself and totally filled with the Holy Spirit as I speak and write. I pray that it is His words I speak and write — not my own. I don't take lightly the opportunities God gives me to minister to couples, which in turn impacts their marriages and lives from that point forward if the Lord allows. I can't do it without Him! There's no way I could stand up in front of people if the Lord didn't em-power me to do what I do! You know, we can't spill out onto others until we're filled to overflowing. I pray when my cup is full and overflowing the

Lord is all that is in the cup, and none of me is left!

The second reason I'm able to stand up and speak is...I have a wife who encourages and believes in me! When I was doing announcements, messing up and learning how to speak in front of people, she was the one there saying, "Go Joe, I believe in you, you can do it." Later on when I was teaching and messing up and learning how to communicate God's word and how to make an impact in couple's lives, she was the one saying, "Go Joe, you can do it." She is my own personal cheerleader. She saw things in me I didn't see in myself. She specifically encouraged me with her words by helping to build my confidence. She also encouraged me by the hand-written notes I would find in my suitcase, bathroom, or in my pants pocket. These reminders were "encouragement reminders" to me that she believed in me. Ladies, let me tell you this, and please hear this loud and clear. The encouragement of my wife is the reason I'm able to do what I do and was able to step out into the unknown. God called me to leave my comfortable corporate job to go into full-time ministry. We went our first 16 months without a pay check. Everything I made went back into the ministry. Those were hard, tough and trying times. I believe with all my heart that I would not be where I am serving the Lord without her admiration, appreciation and respect. You have SO much power and influence...will you use it for the good?

When our family goes to the pool, our boys say things like, "Mommy, look at this. Did I do good? Did I jump high? Did I splash big? Mommy, Mommy, did you see me?" I bet that sounds familiar to a lot of you. Your husband is just like that little boy, except he's in a little bit bigger body. What he's saying to you is, "Honey, look at this. Did I do good? Are you proud of me? Am I a good husband and father?" How does he try to do this? He tries to make more money, buy you nice things, help out around the house, and take out the garbage. If he has stopped doing these things, maybe it is because he feels he doesn't get your admiration, appreciation and respect anymore. Why try if he doesn't get what he so desperately needs. He wants and needs

> *"He wants and needs to know you appreciate him and all he does to provide for you and your family. He wants you to be proud of him."*

to know you appreciate him and all he does to provide for you and your family. He wants you to be proud of him.

I was a very shy person as you read above. When Debbie and I first married, I knew I had to learn to change. I had to learn to talk, listen and communicate with her. I don't buy the excuses of "I can't change," or "It can't be done," or "I've always done it this way," or "I grew up this way," or "My parents were like this." We **CAN** change if we really want to change! I pray you'll let the Holy Spirit work through you and be what He wants you to be instead of what you want to be. You can do it! Make the changes you need to be a better person and a better spouse.

Chapter 19

Stay Attractive To Your Husband

What does it take to turn on your husband? The answer is ANY-THING? The majority of men are aroused visually, so that's why this area is so crucial in your marriage. Since your husband is a visual creature, it is important for you to look good. Remember, for women, it's a mind thing. For men, it's a sight thing. Now, I am not saying you need to look like a model, but you do need to look good and stay attractive to him. Does your husband find you attractive and sexy? You may need to get some updated clothes, a new hairstyle, and/or get on a workout program, because he wants to keep that same attractive lady he first married. Being married doesn't give you an excuse to change dramatically. Just because you have your wedding ring on your finger doesn't mean you don't have to keep working at looking good to him. Some of you may say, "Isn't my husband supposed to love me unconditionally?" The answer is yes; but you cannot base your lack of discipline on that phrase. You don't have to look like you stepped off a magazine cover, but you do need to be attractive to your husband. If you don't look good, he won't look very much!

If your husband picks and pinches you, then you should be glad. If he's doing that it means he's attracted to you. Now guys, I know it's pretty annoying to your wife to be pinched 100 times, so just keep it under 99 and you're okay. Ladies, think about this question when you get annoyed. Would you rather him be picking and pinching you, or picking and pinching another woman? You might say, "Well Joe, since you put it that way, it's not so bad after all." That sort of changes the perspective doesn't it? You need to be thankful he finds you attractive.

My wife and I were at the grocery store and saw a lady in the distance who looked somewhat familiar, but neither of us could place her. She got closer and we said hello, being cordial. Now, the reason we couldn't figure out who she was is because she had on a ball cap w/ greasy hair sticking out of the back, no make-up, no jewelry, and she was wearing a sweat suit with worn out tennis shoes. It didn't dawn on us for several minutes who she really was. We were standing there with our mouths wide open in awe thinking, "Did you take a look in the mirror before you left your house"? Don't get me wrong, it's ok to be a slob every once in a while, but if that is the norm, then this may be something to think about. She looked SO different without make-up—it was amazing. I'm all for natural beauty, and I'm not trying to be superficial. Practically speaking, if your husband is a visual creature, it really is important for your physical appearance to be appealing to him. The ladies at work and the ladies he sees out in public look nice, so he would like you to look nice as well. Just like I shave every day to stay attractive to my wife—Debbie fixes herself up every day as one of the ways she chooses to stay attractive to me. I did not ask that of her. This is something she likes to do for me. Ladies, you know when you are attractive and when you aren't. When you take the time to work on your appearance and take pride in yourself, you look better than when you put on an old ball cap and sweats.

Let's keep all of this in perspective. A wife not only needs to work on improving her outward appearance —she needs to work on her inward appearance. I Peter 3:1-7 talks about this very thing. Verse 4 (NASV) says, "But let it be the hidden person of the heart, with the imperishable quality of a gentle and quiet spirit, which is precious in the sight of God." When my wife was a little girl, her mom would dress her up to the fullest on Sunday mornings like most moms do. There was an elderly lady who would say to her almost every Sunday, "My, you sure do look pretty. Do your insides look as pretty as you look on the outside?" The Lord looks at our heart. The Lord is more concerned about what's on the inside than what is on the outside.

Debbie had a grandmother we called Nana. Nana was one of the most beautiful women I've ever met. Not because of her physical beauty, but because of the radiance that came from the inside and from the Lord. She had a bounce in her step and was always smiling, encouraging, and teasing with people. She had a different perspective than most people. Nana and Papa lived in Michigan and got a lot of snow. She would write a letter to us and say, "It's snowing outside, and it reminds me of how

Jesus washed our sins away as white as snow." That is not the perspective of snow we have. We're thinking, "How fast can they get this stuff off the ground so I can get to where I need to be." She was beautiful on the inside, and it couldn't help but flow to the outside in her attitude and perspective of life. Nana is with the Lord now, but her legacy lives on as she made a permanent impact on our family. One of the things that attracted me to Debbie was her spunk,

> *"If you are beautiful on the inside, it can't help but flow to the outside… in your personality, how you carry yourself and your outlook on life."*

smile, and love for life. She is a lot like her Nana. If you are beautiful on the inside, it can't help but flow to the outside…in your personality, how you carry yourself and your outlook on life.

I learned something new a few months ago. I had always seen the jets flying through the sky high above and leaving a trail behind them. I had thought the trail was smoke from the engines, but I learned differently. The trail they leave is called a contrail which is short for a condensation trail. What appears as smoke is actually a vapor trail. When the hot jet engine hits the cold atmosphere, it creates a vapor trail in the sky. This is why you see the "trail" disappear several minutes after the plane passes overhead. When I see the contrails in the sky, it reminds me how short life really is. We shouldn't go through life with poor attitudes. We need to have a great attitude and an eternal perspective like Nana. The Bible puts it this way in James 4:14, "Yet you do not know what your life will be like tomorrow. You are just a vapor that appears for a little while and then vanishes away." (NASB) This visual reminder in the sky helps me to keep my perspective on eternal things and to remind me of just how precious the time is that God has given me. The next time you look up into the sky and see the contrails, I hope you'll think about this verse and be reminded to live life to the fullest with a great attitude like Nana!

Keeping an eternal perspective in life is more important than focusing on the here and now. As I've noted, our outward appearance shouldn't be our main focus. Staying attractive to your husband is a very important point to keep in mind since God made him a visual creature in his makeup. Will you work to be beautiful on the inside and outside?

Chapter 20

After Work He Needs To Come To A Home...Not A House

You know, there is a distinct difference between a house and a home. A house is just a place to live, but a home is a haven for the entire family. It's a place of safety, fun, and memories. I'm breaking down the word 'home' into an acrostic, and I pray these simple reminders will help you to make your house a home.

H — **Hug** — When your husband gets home, do you show him that you missed him, you're glad to see him and give him a hug? This sets the tone for the entire evening. If you are working on dinner or something else, Stop! Take the time to give him a special hug, look into his eyes, and tell him you're glad he's home. Something as small as a hug as soon as he gets home does wonders for the soul. It shows appreciation, love and value.

O — **Organization** — Do you keep things organized and in order? For couples with small children, you may be thinking, "Yeah, right Joe. How's organized chaos?" That's a start. Your husband needs to be able to unwind and enjoy coming home to order instead of disaster. This helps him look forward to coming home to his little haven of peace and love. He wants you to handle your share of the responsibilities so everyone can share a restful and enjoyable time together. Everyone needs the opportunity to unwind at the end of the day. You can help make this possible for everyone.

"A house is just a place to live, but a home is a haven for the entire family. It's a place of safety, fun, and memories."

If you are a stay at home mom, you need to strive to have toys and clutter picked up when your husband comes home. Try to make it your priority to get the household duties done before your kids and husband come home. Things don't have to be perfect. You shouldn't expect your house to be like something out of 'Leave it to Beaver," but make it a point to get things organized. Pick one task at a time and tackle it. You can do it!

Make sure you haven't volunteered for so much that it pulls you away from your duties as a mom and wife. Some are so involved with outside obligations they let the home duties go by the wayside. Your home and family need to be your first prior-

> **"Your home and family need to be your first priority."**

ity. Debbie even tries to have dinner already made or mostly made before the kids come home from school, and then we can warm it up. This way all attention can be put on homework or whatever needs to be done.

Not once have I ever demanded Debbie to have the house 'picked up' when I get home. (I'm bigger than her, but I can tell you that all of her small 5' 1" frame can take me at any time! Ha-ha) She takes this upon herself. I don't walk in the door and say, "The king is home...where's my robe, slippers, and paper? And by the way, I expect dinner in 10 minutes." Doesn't the thought of that just make the hair on the back of your neck stand up or make your blood pressure rise? Whew! I know this is especially hard with small children, but he needs to be able to unwind and enjoy coming home to order and not to disaster.

M — Mood — Now, I know that most of you men thought this 'M' stood for meal. If you want two 'M's,' knock yourself out. A wife's mood and tone sets the stage for the rest of the evening for the family. A very true expression is, "If mama ain't happy, ain't nobody happy." If you're grumpy, then everyone is going to be grumpy. Creating this atmosphere doesn't fall entirely on the wife's shoulders, but you do play a big part in setting the tone and how it's displayed to the rest of the family.

E — Enjoyment — Do you try to create an enjoyable atmosphere in your home? Does your husband enjoy coming home? Are you so busy trying to take care of everything that you're not taking time to "enjoy" your family? I've written a series titled, "Stop and Smell Your Family... Keeping Your Family a Main Priority." I'm not talking about smelling their underarms or anything like that. What does the expression, "Stop and Smell the Flowers" mean to you? It means stopping the busyness of life long enough to enjoy the life God has given us. You need to stop and take the time to smell the beautiful flowers that God has put right in front of you..."stop and smell" or enjoy your family.

I am frequently asked what I think is the number one thing tearing families apart. That's real easy for me to answer...busyness. Families are so busy that they don't have time to be a family! Busy schedules and activities have taken the place of quality family time like eating together around your table, talking, playing games, playing ball in your back yard or at a park, a picnic at a park, or hiking and laughing to name a few. Are you so busy doing things you don't have time to just be together? Life's busyness and schedules can suck the life out of everyone, and then you don't have time to enjoy those who mean the most to you...your family. **Take the time now to "stop and smell" your family...it's AWESOME!**

Part of that enjoyment is to simply take the time to "hang out" with your family. TV can take away so much time from a family if you allow it. There have been approximately 4,000 studies conducted to examine television's effect on children. The average child spends four hours a day, which equates to 28 hours a week, watching television. To contrast this, the average parent spends 3.5 minutes per week in meaningful conversation with their children.[1] There's a major imbalance going on here. TV may be a way to relax, but as parents, you need to focus on what really matters. Make time for your family or it won't happen on its own. Life's busyness may take the place of your "family time" and you won't be able to get back the time you should have spent together. One day it will be too late. They will be grown and gone. The important thing to remember is that you can make your home a place of enjoyment as you maximize the quality and unhurried time you spend with your family. You can make your house a home by making it a safe haven for the entire family. What changes do you need to make in your house to make it a H-O-M-E?

Notes

1. Statistics taken from internet article (www.csun.edu/science/health/docs/tv&health.html). California State University, Northridge — Norman Herr, Ph.D., according to A.C. Nielsen Co. research.

Application Time — The Irresistible Wife

Men...rank these categories in order of importance to you from 1 to 9. Number 1 will be what is most important to you. Discuss each topic with your wife and explain why this is a priority to you and why it makes you feel loved:

_____ **He needs regular sex.**

What is your spouse currently doing in this area that you like?
....
....
....

What are some suggestions you can give your spouse to improve in this area?
....
....
....

_____ **He needs you to listen and comprehend what he is saying.**

What is your spouse currently doing in this area that you like?
....
....
....

What are some suggestions you can give your spouse to improve in this area?
....
....
....

_____ **Promote him in his career.**

What is your spouse currently doing in this area that you like?
....
....
....

What are some suggestions you can give your spouse to improve in this area?
....
....
....

_____ **Remember, he married you to be his lover, not his mother.**

What is your spouse currently doing in this area that you like?
. . . .
. . . .
. . . .

What are some suggestions you can give your spouse to improve in this area?
. . . .
. . . .
. . . .

_____ **He needs your admiration and appreciation, in other words RESPECT.**

What is your spouse currently doing in this area that you like?
. . . .
. . . .
. . . .

What are some suggestions you can give your spouse to improve in this area?
. . . .
. . . .
. . . .

_____ **Stay attractive to your husband.**

What is your spouse currently doing in this area that you like?
. . . .
. . . .
. . . .

What are some suggestions you can give your spouse to improve in this area?
. . . .
. . . .
. . . .

_____ **After work, he needs to come to a home...not a house.**

What is your spouse currently doing in this area that you like?
. . . .
. . . .
. . . .

What are some suggestions you can give your spouse to improve in this area?

....

....

....

Conclusion

Marriage isn't always 'peachy.' There are hurts and trials we face each and every day. Some need to let go of their hurts and forgive. Some people chain themselves to their hurts—break yourself free and forgive. You need to get it out in the open, you need to admit to those things and ask forgiveness from your spouse. Remember, forgiveness is a two-way street...it's a cycle...it's a process. One person asks forgiveness; the other grants forgiveness. If both parties do their part, that completes the forgiveness cycle. The best example I can give to explain forgiveness is personal. My youngest son, Tucker, is full of energy. He is energy, looking for a place to go. He is full of life, loves living, and is always looking for something to do. He's got that sparkle in his eyes. We were eating breakfast one morning and several things got knocked off the table. I thought it was Tucker and gave him correction. I found out a few minutes later that it wasn't Tucker who made the mess, it was our other son. If you've ever had to apologize to your child, you know how I felt—like a worm. I went to Tucker and said, "Tucker, Dad gave you correction, and you didn't deserve it. I was wrong...Will you forgive me?" What he said was so powerful. We call it 'Tucker Forgiveness.' He said, "Daddy, I forgive you, and I still love you," and then he put out his arms wide to give me a big hug. This dad was pretty wiped out at that point. You know, that's what our Heavenly Father does to us when we mess up and come back to him. He says in essence, I forgive you. My son Jesus paid the price for all of your sins, I still love you, and then His divine arms welcome us back into the right relationship with Him! When Debbie and I ask forgiveness of each other, we do 'Tucker Forgiveness.' When our boys ask forgiveness of each other, they do 'Tucker Forgiveness.' Now, the hug is very important. You can tell if things aren't right if the hug isn't genuine. It is a pretty good indication of what's going on in the heart. We make sure there's a hug, because this physical touch is very important.

Many husbands and wives need to put into practice the forgiveness cycle...one needs to ask forgiveness and the other needs to grant forgiveness. Asking for forgiveness is an event and a process from that event; trust is a process which takes awhile for some of the wounds to heal. It's one thing to say, "I forgive you." It's something else to say, "I still love you." From that point, as a couple, you need to move on to the touch. You can tell from the hug what's in the heart.

Have you ever gone to the beach and drawn a line in the sand? What happens to that line after the waves keep coming up over it? It gets washed away. Think of the commitment in your marriage as that line. Maybe the waves of life and busyness have been washing over this line and eroding the commitment in your marriage that once was so strong. Have you told your spouse you are there for him or her, no matter what, and that you are going to make your marriage work?

If you drive a car looking in the rear view mirror only, you're going to wreck. You are so focused on what's behind you that you can't see and appreciate what's in front of you. If you continue to live in the past it will sabotage your future. What some of you need to do is rip off the rear view mirror of your past, throw it out the window, and say to yourself and to your spouse, "By God's grace, we're not going back there anymore. We are focusing on the future and the blessings God has given to us." Quit living in the past and admit that you can change. Realize if you keep driving your life while looking in the rear view mirror, you are going to wreck. You have to look forward in your marriage and in your life. You can't change the past, but you can change your future course!

"Father, I come to you in Jesus' name and I thank you for the time we can spend together through this book. Lord I thank you so much for married couples and for their time and commitment to read this book. I pray this experience will be a line in the sand for many. I pray you will provide healing, restoration and enrichment. I give you the honor and glory for all that has been said and done. Lord, we are nothing without you. We give you the praise for everything. I thank you so much for creating us man and woman, for putting us together, and giving us the joy of being able to live with our best friend, our spouse. Lord, thank you for creating a plan for how we can be "Hooked for Life." In Jesus' name, I pray. Amen."